Pondering Another Passage

A. C. Gray

Pondering Another Passage

Printed in the United States of America

Packaged by WinePress Publishing, PO Box 428, Enumclaw, WA 98022. The views expressed or implied in this work do not necessarily reflect those of WinePress Publishing. Ultimate design, content, and editorial accuracy of this work are the responsibilities of the author.

ISBN #1-57921-299-9
LCCN: 00–102410

Manufactured in the United States of America

By the same author:

Pondering My Passage: A Spiritual Odyssey
American Literary Press, 1995

The author welcomes correspondence:

A. C. Gray
Arbreux – 35 Deerlick Lane
Broadway, VA 22815-5006

Email: Arbreux@hotmail.com

Gratitude

My thanks go to Master Captain Ulf E. Mahnke and the entire crew of the Cho Yang Atlas for their warm hospitality during my sojourn aboard the ship. Their names are listed at the end of the book. Special thanks go to Wesley M. (Pat) Pattillo for his encouragement, for reading and skillfully editing this manuscript for the World Wide Web, and for using his computer skills to update the log of my voyage as I progressed around the planet. Gratitude beyond measure goes to Jack Brammer for encouraging me at the outset to give God the glory at every opportunity.

I am also indebted to Muriel and Lester Bittel for reading the manuscript and enthusiastically encouraging me to proceed with publication.

Carter Wiecking's professional review, suggestions, and encouragement brought about a more readable manuscript. Warm appreciation, too, goes to Chuck and Athena Dean at WinePress for their authentic Christian witness and encouragement, and to Marjie Long who skillfully and professionally managed the production of this book. Thanks also go to Ty Rogel who designed the cover in the diary format and to Nik Baumgart who superbly set the type. An extended family of friends traveled with me in spirit with their support and prayers.

A. C. Gray
Arbreux, April 30, 2000

Embarkation

Dear Reader:

This book records the continuation of a spiritual odyssey recorded in my memoir, *Pondering My Passage*. It is both an account of my journey around the world, most of the way via a modern containership, and an account of my spiritual voyage. From the moment we lifted anchor in Long Beach, California I found myself on an adventure that recalled much of the geography of my past travels and many of the biblical stories that were stored in my memory, prompting me to read them again and ponder their meaning anew.

I would be passing where Moses and the children of Israel made their Exodus from Egypt as they crossed the Red Sea. In the Mediterranean I would pass Malta, where the apostle Paul was shipwrecked. As we passed Turkey to our north I would recall the great flood and Noah's arc coming to rest on Mount Ararat. These and other stories from the Bible would come alive and have fresh new meaning as I passed in review the great epics of history.

In my luggage was my most valuable item of cargo, not only for this voyage, but also for life. It was a small edition of *The Holy Bible.* It became a prism through which I focused my thoughts even as it has become a lamp post through which my world and my life have been illumined with the awesome majesty and love of God.

In this volume I share the verses of Scripture that I recorded daily in my journal. I found myself captivated with how often the sea and its many moods were recorded as metaphors in the Bible. One supreme message came through all my meditations, centered in three words of Jesus: *It is written.*

I had a compelling need to share the Scriptures and thoughts that derived from them. So I have transcribed them here with hope that all who read them might share in my spiritual journey. Within God's Word are the promises and assurances of all I shall ever need. Dear reader, I pray that you will be blessed by reading these selected verses and thoughts scattered through these pages as I logged them daily along the ocean beltway of our planet.

The Bible's use of the ocean voyage as a metaphor for life's voyage provides a fitting perspective for the brevity of our days. Recently a friend's sudden need for brain microsurgery reminded me anew that we do not have forever to express our faith, our love for one another, or our requests for forgiveness where need be. We travel through life, each of us, in small boats on very turbulent seas, some of us more tempest-tossed than others. How well we cope with life's troubled waters depends upon our faith and upon whom we choose to captain our souls. If the Master of our voyage is Jesus Christ, we can be certain that our ship will be brought to safe harbors. Amy Carmichael captured this theme in poetic verse:

> Thou art the Lord who slept upon the pillow,
> Thou art the Lord who soothed the furious sea,
> What matter the beating wind and tossing billow
> If only we are in the boat with Thee?
>
> Hold us in quiet through the age-long minute
> While Thou art silent, and the wind is still:
> Can the boat sink while Thou, dear Lord, art in it?
> Can the heart faint that waiteth on Thy will?*

A. C. Gray,
Arbreux, March 2, 2000

---

*Amy Carmichael, "The Age-Long Minute"

Others went out on the sea in ships; they were merchants on the mighty waters. They saw the works of the Lord, His wonderful deeds in the deep. For He spoke and stirred up a tempest that lifted high the waves. They mounted up to the heavens and went down to the depths; in their peril their courage melted away. They reeled and staggered like drunken men; they were at their wits end. Then they cried out to the Lord in their trouble, and He brought them out of their distress. He stilled the storm to a whisper; the waves of the sea were hushed. They were glad when it grew calm, and He guided them to their desired haven. Let them give thanks to the Lord for His unfailing love and His wonderful deeds for men.

Psalm 107:23:31

A voyage is a piece of autobiography at best.

Robert Louis Stevenson, The Cevennes Journal

The shortest way to yourself is a journey around the world.

Graf Keyserling

A good traveler has no fixed plans, and is not intent upon arriving.

Lao Tzu

One does not discover new lands without consenting to lose sight of the shore for a very long time.

Andre Gide

It is 1930 hours and the giant containership *Cho Yang Atlas* is maneuvering its way into its berth at Rotterdam. I hear the now familiar groans of its cargo of more than 4,000 containers straining at their moorings, the slapping of swells against the starboard hull, and the heartbeat of the mammoth diesel engines propelling the rudder. In just a short while unloading will begin at this vast dock, one of the largest in the world, where blazing lights illuminate giant overhead cranes on railways and a fleet of waiting trucks. This will be the first full service stop since we left Singapore eighteen days ago, pausing only overnight in the Red Sea to refuel before transiting the Suez Canal. There are only two more stops on my journey before leaving the ship in Felixstowe, England just four days hence. And my voyage of more than 18,000 nautical miles will have come to an end.

There is a sense in which each day is a voyage in which we make a passage from being a different person from the one we were the day before. This is not a clairvoyant insight, for we all know that we are daily becoming someone different. However, some voyages are longer and more dramatic. Such has been this one. I was prepared to relearn how to play bridge with other passengers, to watch videos, to exchange anecdotes and vignettes with fellow travelers, but none of this occurred because I found myself the sole passenger. So, much of my time was spent reading good books, keeping a log, and writing long letters.

I think I must have had a subconscious wish to be the only passenger because I wanted this voyage to be life changing. I know that I wanted to trade the routine humdrum and ordinary days for something extraordinary. The Psalmist had given me courage and hope long ago when I secretly wished to make a voyage around the world on a freighter: "Delight yourself in the Lord and He will give you the desires of your heart" (Ps. 37:4). I wanted to know at the end of the journey that the time and resources invested had been worthwhile. I wanted to know that I had made a passage to being a better person than I was when I left. I now want that idea as a lifetime *mindset*: to think of each new day as a voyage to becoming a new and better me.

In her book *Gift from the Sea,* Anne Morrow Lindbergh wrote that one cannot collect all the beautiful shells on the beach. One can collect only a few and if they are few, they are more beautiful. In the same way we can clutter our lives with too many activities, too many valuable things, and even too many interesting people. We must be selective if we would make room for the best. On this voyage I have had the gift of solitude to ponder and select a few exquisite everlasting treasures: a renewed reverence for all Creation, a rediscovery of worship and wonder, and a soul-satisfying joy of communion with the Creator. In this book, I simply hope to share some of these gifts.

All this year I have been transcribing verses of Scripture to the zippered address book that goes with me everywhere. Writing them out in longhand helps me fix in mind the special wisdom they speak, and perhaps deters my brain for a little while from its certain dementia. I have also incorporated them into the log of this voyage, for my passage has been one of the spirit as well as the body. Yesterday I read through them and chose one to use on the scrolling marquee screen saver on my computer. This was the apostle Paul writing to the Romans (9:16): "It does not depend on man's desire or effort, but on God's mercy." That verse has multiple meanings, but for the purpose of these pages, God's mercy has been sufficient and abundant. To Him be the glory.

acg

Rotterdam, October 3, 1999

Mr. Phileas Fogg lived, in 1872, at No. 7, Saville Row, Burlington Gardens, the house in which Sheridan died in 1814. He was one of the most noticeable members of the Reform Club, though he seemed always to avoid attracting attention; an enigmatical person about whom little was known, he was a polished man of the world. . . . Had he traveled? It was likely, for no one seemed to know the world more familiarly; there was no spot so secluded that he did not appear to have an intimate acquaintance with it. He often corrected, with a few clear words, the thousand conjectures advanced by members of the club as to lost and unheard-of travelers, pointing out the true probabilities, and seeming gifted with a sort of second sight. He must have traveled everywhere, at least in spirit.

Around the World in Eighty Days
—Jules Verne

Awaiting Arrival of the Cho Yang Atlas

> The Lord will keep you from all harms. . . . He will watch over your life: the Lord will watch over your coming and going both now and forevermore. (Ps. 121:8 THE TRAVELER'S PSALM)[1]

August 21, 1999

> The fear of the Lord is the beginning of knowledge . . . but whoever listens to me will live in safety and be at ease, without fear of harm. (Prov. 1:7, 33)

I decided to read one chapter of Proverbs every day and choose a verse from each chapter that speaks directly to

1. Scripture quotes were taken from *the New International Version of the Holy Bible, except where otherwise noted. Please note also that all pronouns with reference to God have been capitalized.*

me. So I accept today's Scripture as an admonition and omen as I begin this journey around the world . . . with deepest gratitude for the measure of good health and the means whereby I am enabled. I shall read other Scriptures as well. My thoughts turn to the distressing disaster of western Turkey's earthquake. It reminds me altogether of life's fragile balance and our common brotherhood with people all over our world.

August 22, 1999—Long Beach, California

I am about one tenth of my way around the world and awaiting arrival of the Cho Yang Atlas.

> For the Lord gives wisdom: and from His mouth come knowledge and understanding. (Prov. 2:6)

> By wisdom the Lord laid the earth's foundations, by understanding he set the heavens in place; by His knowledge the deeps were divided, and the clouds let drop the dew. (Prov. 3:19)

I am reading Peter Nichols' *Sea Change*, an account of his solo voyage across the Atlantic in a wooden boat. He talks about navigating by the stars and sensing as he does so the touch of divine creation. It is an adventure story and ends with his being rescued by a container ship after his sailboat disintegrates at sea near Bermuda. At the same time, I have been reading Dava Sobel's *Longitude*, a gift from Eva DeCourcey and the best-seller story of how an eccentric genius of Britain, John Harrison, developed clocks that correctly divided time into 24 segments, all synchronized with movement of the planets and stars. So these scriptures from Proverbs fit perfectly with my mindset.

August 23, 1999—Long Beach, California

This afternoon, I found four more books at Acres of Books, a "used" bookstore in Long Beach. Among them: Fyodor Dostoyevsky's *The Brothers Karamazov*. Maybe I'll have the time to absorb it completely aboard ship, my second "go" at this masterpiece of literature. Another book has the provocative title, *When All You've Ever Wanted Isn't Enough*, by Harold Kushner. The subtitle is The Search for a Life that Matters. I end this day pondering this quote from Kushner:

> Our souls are not hungry for fame, comfort, wealth, or power. Those rewards create almost as many problems as they solve. Our souls are hungry for meaning, for the sense that we have figured out how to live so that our lives matter, so that the world will be at least a little bit different for our having passed through it.[2]

I close my day with a prayer that I might find meaning in sharing this log with hundreds of friends around the world, enabling them to catch a glimpse of the wonder and magnificence of this fragile planet on which we are all passengers . . . that in some very small way it will have made a difference that I made my way around it once more.

> Therefore, we ought to give the more earnest heed to the things, which we have heard, lest at any time we should let them slip. (Heb. 2:1)

These verses from Scripture remind me that the Bible is God's Word, speaking directly to those who take it seriously. And with each reading of the same text comes a contemporary

2. Harold Kushner, *When All You've Ever Wanted Isn't Enough.* New York: Simon & Schuster, 1985 , p. 18. Used by permission.

and fresh new message. I choose to believe this because it seems to have been my experience repeatedly.

Aboard the Cho Yang Atlas

August 24, 1999—Long Beach, California

> The greatest reward of sailing alone . . . is that no one comes between you and the indescribably beautiful world around you. You experience it directly without the muddying filter of someone else's impression. At moments, standing on deck looking at the lonely sea and the sky, you find yourself moved to a mixed joy and sadness that breaks your heart. But it's at just these moments that you also find yourself wanting to share it all with someone you love.[3]
>
> *Sea Change*
> —Peter Nichols

I boarded the Cho Yang Atlas this afternoon although the ship will not depart until tomorrow. Meanwhile, around the clock, containers are being unloaded, enough to supply dozens of Wal-Marts, K-marts, and Costcos. Each container is about the size of a trailer you would see on a eighteen wheeler on the Interstate! These contain American products that will go to Taiwan, China, and Malaysia, all a part of what you hear discussed in the news as our balance of trade. I am resigned to hearing the steady drum of the loading cadence all night long, although the noise is nicely muffled here in the cabin.

At the outset, it is interesting to note that more than ninety percent of the world's commerce is transported from one part of the world to another on container ships.

3. Peter Nichols, *Sea Change*. London: Penguin Books, 1997., p.162. Used by permission.

Altogether, there are more than 40,000 freighters now on the high seas. Although I will be sailing most of the way around the world and on the busiest sea routes, I will see only a fraction of the total. Also, for Americans, almost everything purchased in any store will have been transported, either as raw materials or as packaged finished goods, sometime on a container ship. Nearly the only exception is food items, which, for the most part, are exports. Even American automobiles are assembled packages of foreign-made parts and furnishings. Automobiles, trucks, and heavy equipment machinery are also transported from one part of the world to another on freighters, called "Ro-Ros", for "roll-on, roll-off." At sea a Ro-Ro looks like a gigantic garage on the superstructure of a ship.

I am now ensconced in a cabin labeled "Spare Officer—2" which has a living room furnished with a couch and two chairs, nice desk, mini-refrigerator, VCR, and Panasonic entertainment center; a bedroom with two beds; and bathroom. The ship has central air conditioning, which makes life indoors very pleasant with the outside temperature in the high nineties.

Master Ulf E. Mahnke captains this ship with a crew of twenty-one, of whom five, including himself, are German, five are Filipino, and eleven are Kiribati. I, with my birthday and passport number, am registered along with the others on the crew list as a supernumerary. I am the oldest person aboard and the only passenger—and think of myself the youngest at heart! Peter Pieper, the chief engineer and a German, is next oldest at 60.

This vacation at sea has been a deliberate choice. On so many of my other journeys, the experience of travel itself has been an adjunct of work, opening my perspective to all things new. On this voyage I choose to ponder the foundations, the deeps, the clouds dropping dew, and the heavens in place. And I take seriously Anne Morrow Lindbergh's admonition for patience, waiting with open hands and an open heart for a gift from the sea. The greatest gifts of life are the intangibles.

August 25, 1999

> By wisdom the Lord laid the foundations, by understanding he set the heavens in place; by his knowledge the deeps were divided, and the clouds let drop the dew. (Prov. 3:19)

> The sea does not reward those who are too anxious, too greedy, or too impatient. To dig for treasures, shows not only impatience and greed but lack of faith. Patience, patience, patience is what the sea teaches. Patience and faith. One should lie empty, open, choiceless as a beach—waiting for a gift from the sea.[4]
>
> *Gift from the Sea*
> —Anne Morrow Lindbergh

We sail today! Of course, we don't sail, but such is the nautical term for moving even giant ships like this one. Though I am just a passenger, I await our sailing this afternoon with great anticipation. I recall lines by T. S. Eliot in "Little Gidding" from Four Quartets:

> We shall not cease from exploration
> And the end of our exploring
> Will be to arrive where we started
> And know the place for the first time.

4. Anne Morrow Lindbergh, *Gift from the Sea*. New York: Signet Books, 1957. p.17. Used by permission.

Eliot captured my own experience and response to travel. All my journeys, for official duties and otherwise, have ended with my having a deeper appreciation of wherever I called "home" at the time. But more, they have ended with a renewed appreciation of life itself, for the gifts of good health, intellectual curiosity, and a measure of mental soundness for comparing my lot in life with others. I've always returned home with a greater measure of appreciation for all my many blessings. This is a theme about which I could write a book!

The container terminal at Long Beach is a vast beehive of tractor-trailer trucks arriving and departing from shipside. Imagine this: more than 4,000 trucks will have arrived to either load or unload containers during the two days the Cho Yang Atlas is in port. The ship itself sits under four gigantic cranes, equipped with a trolley-driven, air-conditioned, glass-enclosed operator cage that slides back and forth, picking up and dropping containers on the ship. I observed the loading process for a long time this morning. To an observer the process has a mystery about it of an anthill in the making; yet logisticians have perfected the efficiency of loading these giant ships with their computers. Captain Mahnke told me this morning at breakfast that the precise location and destination of every container is known at any moment in time. "What do they contain?" I asked. "You take a guess and my answer will be 'yes,' because they contain everything that moves in commerce except illegal drugs and explosives."

But the only true travelers are those who leave
For the sake of leaving; with hearts light as balloons,
They never deviate from their destiny,
And not knowing why, they always say, Let's go!

The Voyage

—Charles Baudelaire

In my portfolio for this voyage I placed this piece by Wilford A. Peterson entitled The Art of Traveling. It is worth sharing.

> When you pack your bags to explore the beauties of your own country or to travel around the world, consider these keys to a happy journey:
>
> - Travel lightly. You are not traveling for people to see you!
> - Travel slowly. Jet planes are for getting places not seeing places. Take time to absorb the beauty and inspiration of a mountain or a cathedral.
> - Travel expectantly. Every place you visit is like a surprise package to be opened. Untie the strings with an expectation of high adventure.
> - Travel hopefully. "To travel hopefully," wrote Robert Louis Stevenson, "is better than to survive."
> - Travel humbly. Visit people and places with reverence and respect for their traditions and ways of life.
> - Travel courteously. Consideration for your fellow travelers and your hosts will smooth the way through the most difficult days.
> - Travel gratefully. Show appreciation for the many things that are being done by others for your enjoyment and comfort.
> - Travel with an open mind. Leave your prejudices at home.

- Travel with curiosity. It is not how far you go, but how deeply you go that mines the gold of experience. Thoreau wrote a big book about Walden Pond.

- Travel with imagination. As the Old Spanish proverb puts it: "He who would bring home the wealth of the Indies must carry the wealth of the Indies with him."

- Travel fearlessly. Banish worry and timidity; the world and its people belong to you just as you belong to the world.

- Travel relaxed. Make up your mind to have a good time. Let go and let God.

- Travel patiently. It takes time to understand others, especially when there are barriers of language and custom; keep flexible and adaptable to all situations.

- Travel with the spirit of a world citizen. You'll discover that people are basically the same the world around. Be an ambassador of good will to all people.

Underway

August 25, 1999

We pulled away from Long Beach Pier A22 at 1825, just a little over an hour ago. I was on the bridge deck as the ship was maneuvered through a narrow channel to the open sea, assisted by a pilot boat. We passed a number of ships flying Liberian and Panamian flags of registry. Ours, however, proudly waves the registry flag of a reunified Germany. I sensed that sailors on the other ships viewed the Cho Yang Atlas as having an enormous amount of prestige in the maritime world, not only because it has German registry, but because the ship is also enormous and new.

In the Long Beach harbor sits the proud Queen Mary that once held the speed record for Atlantic crossings, so large that it could not transit the Panama Canal, and 137 feet longer than the Titanic. We are underway now at a speed of about 20 knots. The dead weight and size of the ship now in relatively calm waters results in only a slightly rolling motion. I'll be rocked to sleep tonight.

Sailing time to San Francisco/Oakland is just sixteen hours. So I will be awake and on deck when we arrive in San Francisco bay and dock in Oakland tomorrow morning at about 0900.

> The need for meaning is not a biological need like the need for food and air. Neither is it a psychological need, like the need for acceptance and self-esteem. It is a religious need, an ultimate thirst of our souls.
>
> *When All You've Ever Wanted Isn't Enough*
>
> —Harold Kushner

August 26, 1999

Ralph W. Seager provides my meditation for this morning with his abbreviated essay:

The Extravagance of God

More sky than man can see,
More seas than he can sail,

More sun than he can bear to watch,
More stars than he can scale.
More breath than he can breathe,
More yield than he can sow
More grace than he can comprehend
More love than he can know.

The last time I arrived in San Francisco by ship was nearly 30 years ago, in November 1969. I was returning home from fifteen months of Air Force duty at Wakkanai, Hokkaido, Japan. We sailed under the Golden Gate Bridge on the USS President Cleveland at dawn in dense fog, and many American passengers were on deck for our homecoming. When we had departed Yokohama, Japan the band played "San Francisco, Here I Come." Many passengers were diplomats returning from postings in Vietnam, Burma, Laos, Thailand, and Cambodia. The camaraderie and joy of being home in America for Christmas this year was contagious.

The predictable early morning fog in San Francisco is here again today, but overhead the clouds are dispersing and the sky is blue, an encouraging omen for our short stop, only ten hours. However, the captain informed me that we must anchor until tomorrow morning and wait our turn at port. So I shall be content and enjoy my windows on the gateway city. My cabin has two large windows facing starboard and two facing forward with unobstructed views.

I must admit that I love the mountains, but many times I have wondered how different my life might have been had I joined the Navy rather than the Air Force. I have always had wanderlust; anyone who knows me knows that. The yearning to climb aboard a boat, a yacht, or a ship has always been keen for me whenever I am near water, but especially at the seashore. I am fortunate that my view tonight is directly across the bay to San Francisco's skyline.

The water ripples gently and changes colors as the evening cloud formations interact with the setting sun in tones of ivory, pink, rust, gray, and green. As the sun drops out of the sky over the Oakland-Bay Bridge, the horizon blushes in many shades of pink and orange, and the water mirrors the spectacle. I recall the magic of similar sunsets when I lived at Wakkanai, Japan, where the sea was visible from my West-facing bedroom window.

Gulls patrol the bay in formation down toward Alcatraz and Treasure Island. A sailboat meanders slowly by. The dusk begins to sparkle with lights on shore and on other ships anchored in the harbor. These times call for long, long thoughts and give the sea a mystic quality. It is a benediction to be alone while on shore the city bustles with activity. It is good to have this time apart to meditate and to ponder life's wonders and mysteries with no pressing demands, no schedules to meet, no responsibilities. This is what I bargained for when I began the search for a ship.

August 26, 1999—Oakland/San Francisco

In a little while, after breakfast, I will take my walk around the island that is presently my home, the Cho Yang Atlas. It is a fitting metaphor for our ship. The ship is also a fully operating village with electricity; its own water purifying plant, and sewer system. Population only 22 just now, including me. The skyline of San Francisco keeps shifting as the ship makes a pendulum rotation at anchorage. The sky is clear this morning and there's only a faint wisp of fog at the shoreline, a mile or so away.

The day is coming to a close now. Our port arrival was delayed until only a few minutes ago. Word now is that we will not leave until tomorrow afternoon. We will head directly across the Pacific and pass just North of Hawaii en route to Kaohsiung, Taiwan. Captain Mahnke informs me that only in the United States must ships wait port arrival and deal with delayed loading operations.

Just now we are anchored directly facing the Oakland-San Francisco Bay Bridge, and from my window I can see heavy traffic moving both ways on the double decks of the bridge. When darkness falls, it will form a delicate necklace of sparkling headlights on the horizon.

August 27, 1999

Wisdom's call from Proverbs 8:24–29 provides my meditation this morning:

> When there were no oceans, I was given birth, when there were no springs abounding with water; before the mountains were settled in place, before the hills, I was given birth, before He made the earth or its fields or any of the dust of the world. I was there when He set the heavens in place, when He marked out the horizon in the face of the deep, when He established the clouds above and fixed securely the fountains of the deep, when He gave the sea its boundary so the waters would not overstep His command, and when He marked out the foundations of the earth.

A heavy cloud cover hangs over the Bay area this Saturday morning. Another container ship just moved slowly under the Bay Bridge. From my starboard windows I can see Treasure Island, and when we leave today my cabin's forward windows will face directly the Golden Gate Bridge and Treasure Island. But when we pass under the bridge and glide past Alcatraz I will be on deck to bid America Sayonara. Next stop—Kaohsiung, Taiwan eleven days hence on or about September 8.

August 28, 1999

Favorite lines of rhyme and prose theme the philosophical metaphors of life as a traveler or voyage at sea; here are some:

Yonder the long horizon lies, and there by night and day
The old ships draw me home again, and the young ships sail away;
And come I may, but go I must, and if men ask me why,
You may put the blame on the stars
and the sun and the white road and the sky!

Wanderlust
—Gerald Gould

The world stands out on either side
No wider than the heart is wide;
Above the world is stretched the sky-
No higher than the soul is high.
The heart can push the sea and land
Further away on either hand;
The soul can split the sky in two,
And let the face of God shine through.
But East and West will pinch the heart
That cannot keep them pushed apart;
And he whose soul is flat—the sky
Will cave in on him by and by.

Edna St. Vincent Millay

Let me but live my life from year to year,
With forward face and unreluctant soul;
Not hurrying to, nor turning from, the goal;
Not mourning for things that disappear. . . .
In the dim past, not holding back in fear
From what the future veils; but with a whole

And happy heart, that pays its toll to Youth and Age,
And travels on with cheer.
So let the way wind up the hill and down
O'er rough or smooth, the journey shall be joy;
Still seeking what I sought when but a boy,
New friendship, high adventure, and a crown,
My heart will keep the courage of the quest,
And hope the road's last turn will be the best.

The Three Best Things
—Henry van Dyke

At the heart of the cyclone tearing the sky
And flinging the clouds and towers by
Is a place of central calm;
So here in the roar of mortal things,
I have a place where my spirit sings,
In the hollow of God's palm.

The Place of Peace
—Edwin Markham

Fierce was the wild billow,
Dark was the night,
Oars labored heavily,
Foam glittered white;
Trembled the mariners,
Peril was nigh;
Then said the God of God,
"Peace! It is I."

Anatolius, 8th Century

Here is the Truth in a little creed,
Enough for all the roads we go:
In Love is all the law we need,
In Christ is all the God we know.

Quatrain
—Edwin Markham

> When gliding by the Bashee isles we emerged at last upon the great South Sea: were it not for other things, I could have greeted my dear Pacific with uncounted thanks, for now the long supplication of my youth was answered; that serene ocean rolled eastwards from me a thousand leagues of blue. There is, one knows not what sweet mystery about this sea, whose gently awful stirrings seem to speak of some hidden soul beneath; like those fabled undulations of the Ephesian sod over the buried Evangelist St. John. And meet it is, that over these sea-pastures, wide-rolling watery prairies and Potters' Fields of all four continents, the waves should rise and fall, and ebb and flow unceasingly; for here, millions of mixed shades of shadows, drowned dreams, somnambulisms, reveries; all that we call lives and souls, lie dreaming, dreaming, still; tossing like slumberers in their beds; the ever-rolling waves but made so by their restlessness.[5]
>
> *Moby Dick*
>
> —Herman Melville

It is 2000 hours at sea and we are underway to Kaohsiung. We passed under the Golden Gate Bridge about 1830 with the onset of dusk and gathering clouds. The ship has a gentle roll and it will rock me to sleep tonight. Eleven days at sea before we reach Taiwan!

August 29, 1999

> Commit to the Lord whatever you do, and your plans will succeed. (Prov. 16:3)
>
> The moving Moon went up the sky;
> And nowhere did abide:

5. Herman Melville, *Moby Dick*. London: Penguin Books, 1851. p. 456. Copyright expired.

Softly she was going up,
And a star or two beside.

The Rime of the Ancient Mariner
—Samuel Taylor Coleridge

Now comes the challenge of determining where one is on the planet. At sea, mariners now depend on modern electronics and satellites to tell them where they are, but the whole science of determining latitude and longitude depends wholly on the reliability of the heavenly bodies. Consider this brief essay from Dava Sobel's *Longitude*:

> The moving moon, full, gibbous, or crescent-shaped, shone at last for the navigators of the eighteenth century like a luminous hand on the clock of heaven. The broad expanse of sky served as dial for this celestial clock, while the sun, the planets, and the stars painted the numbers on its face.
>
> A seaman could not read the clock of heaven with a quick glance but only with complex observing instruments, with combinations of sightings taken together and repeated as many as seven times in a row for accuracy's sake, and with logarithm tables compiled far in advance by human computers for the convenience of sailors on long voyages. It took about four hours to calculate the time from the heavenly dial—when the weather was clear, that is. If clouds appeared, the clock hid behind them.[6]

Each day now we will be setting the clock back by one hour, thus gaining an extra hour until we reach the International Date Line, when we will jump forward and miss a full day on the calendar. I've made a quick calculation and

6. Dava Sobel, *Longitude*. New York: Walker & Co., 1995, pp 88–89. Used by permission.

believe that this year September 3 will be erased from my calendar. But the days before and the days afterward, as I make my way around the world, will add up to twenty-four hours altogether! Such is this "clock of heaven" that is so dependable we can set our atomic clocks by it.

Johannes Kepler knew this, of course, back in the eighteenth century and even went so far as to suggest that such was the precision of the planets and constellations that, mathematically, their movements constituted a heavenly music, an exquisitely grand symphony. His spirit was so much in sync with the heavenly clock that he set out to prove it with complex geometric notes plotted on a musical scale. So far as I know, no one has proven him wrong. One speculates about the music he may have heard or thought he heard. Was it like a Strauss waltz? Or could it have been some of the restrained notes of what we now think of as "new age," which therapists use in massage sessions? Or was it something more akin to Elgar's Pomp and Circumstance march that graduates hear? Or might it have been like the grand overture to Aida? More likely, I suspect, it would have been for Kepler evocative of one of the great hymns of the church played at St. Paul's or Westminster. Whatever, it is heartwarming to believe that such heavenly harmony does exist and that for those whose final home will be in heaven, we will all hear it someday in eternity.

As far as knowing where we are, sailors can now reliably place their faith in the Global Positioning System (GPS), whereby a system of satellites (artificial stars or moons) are used as focal points to calculate exact longitude and latitude location.

It has been raining out here in the Pacific this morning and my thoughts are with friends back in the Shenandoah

Valley, hoping they, too, are getting some rain. The clouds around the ship have lifted, however, and from my cabin windows on what would be equivalent to the twelfth floor of a fifteen-floor apartment building, I can visually sweep the horizon for some 120 degrees and see that it is still raining in places nearby.

I had an interesting conversation with my cabin steward this morning. His name is Kaiteie Teaotai and he was born at Abemama, Kiribati, in what is better known in America as the Gilbert Islands. Now an independent democracy, the islands still consider themselves a British Commonwealth nation. Kaiteie told me that as a young lad, Prince Charles spent nearly a year there and that people remember playing with him on the beaches. On his island, Kaiteie remembers there being only four automobiles but many bicycles. There are no paved roads. The Germans, in search of cheap labor for their shipping industry, established a marine academy in Kiribati and thus many young men have found careers at sea. The men have contracts for ship duty for durations of up to two years before they can return to their country for home leave. After three to six months of home leave, they leave again for sea duty. It is a noble and sacrificial career and all of the young men on this ship appear to be dedicated and hard workers.

It is instructive to note that although Great Britain once "ruled the waves," the Germans now have dominance in marine shipping. The Danish Line Maersk also has ships that literally traverse the globe. Most of their ships are named for some member of the Maersk family. Yesterday in Oakland I saw the Margarete Maersk and the Gerte Maersk, both containerliners. Captain Mahnke joked that the young people in the Maersk family are encouraged to marry as teenagers and have children as quickly as possible so that the growing fleet of ships could be named. Regrettably, I believe, the United States no longer competes in marine shipping. Recent reports were that Sea-Land and American President Lines were being incorporated into foreign conglomerates. All of this is attributed to unreasonable demands of American labor unions that have literally bargained their members out of meaningful work and livelihoods.

This afternoon I took my first walk around the main deck while the ship was moving. Near the forecastle you have the sensation that you are walking on a live earthquake. Just a bit unstable under foot! I would have done more laps, but the deck was still wet from earlier rain, so I curtailed my exercise. However, I'll try to compensate with a longer swim this afternoon—not in the ocean, but in the pool!

I am reading for the second time Robin Lee Graham's book *Dove*, the story of his incredible solo, five-year voyage around the world on a small yacht, beginning at the age of sixteen. It was chronicled at the time in National Geographic and the story was made into a motion picture. He began his voyage in 1965, so he would be fifty years old now. One of the first places he visited was Upola in Samoa, the adopted home of Robert Louis Stevenson. Famous lines from his poetry, a Requiem, are carved there on Stephenson's stone tomb:

> Home is the sailor, home from the sea,
> And the hunter home from the hill.

August 30, 1999

> The earth is the Lord's and everything in it, the world, and all who live in it. For He founded it upon the seas and established it upon the waters. Psalm 24:1

Yesterday in the passengers' dayroom I found a paperback copy of Herman Melville's *Moby Dick*, the great classic novel about Captain Ahab, Queequeg, and their insane pursuit of a fierce white whale. Among Ahab's crew is Ishmael, a young man undergoing a grueling rite of passage and pursuing a different salvation. Ishmael, like me, was inflicted somewhat by wanderlust. Here's how the novel begins:

> Call me Ishmael. Some years ago—never mind how long precisely—having little or no money in my purse, and nothing particular to interest me on shore, I thought I would sail about a little and see the watery part of the world. . . . Whenever I find myself growing grim about the mouth; whenever it is damp, drizzly November in my soul . . . then I account it high time to get to sea as soon as I can. . . . With a philosophical flourish, Cato throws himself upon his sword; I quietly take to the ship. There is nothing surprising in this. If they but knew it, almost all men in their degree, some time or other, cherish very nearly the same feelings toward the ocean with me.[7]

We are sailing this morning under fair skies and a very calm (pacific) ocean. Fluffy cumulous clouds greeted us at dawn with a three-quarter moon directly overhead. Last night a full moon starboard provided light for my cabin, but the moon's brightness obscured most everything else in the heavens. This morning I walked the sunny side of the ship back and forth. Because of the reefers (refrigerator containers) on the back of the ship now, I can't do a complete circle. Later, after a swim, I sat in a corner of E-deck and soaked up some rays and watched the horizon for any

7. Herman Melville, *Moby Dick*. London: Penguin Books, 1851, p. 21. Copyright expired.

sign of life. From there I could sweep the blue marble of ocean for 270 degrees, but today no ships, no dolphins, no whales. Just a curved horizon as far as you can see. You can actually see the curve of the earth from a ship's deck when there is nothing but sky and water on the horizon.

> And God said, Let the waters bring forth abundantly the moving creatures that hath life, and fowl that may fly above the earth in the open firmament of heaven.
>
> And God created great whales, and every living creature that moveth, which the waters brought forth abundantly, after their kind, and every winged fowl after his kind; and God saw that it was good.
>
> And God blessed them, saying, Be fruitful, and multiply, and fill the waters in the seas, and let fowl multiply in the earth.
>
> And God said, Let us make man in our image, after our likeness: and let them have dominion over the fish of the sea, and over the fowl of the air, and over the cattle, and over all the earth, and over every creeping thing that creepeth upon earth.
>
> So God created man in His own image, in the image of God created He him; male and female created He them. And God blessed them, and God said unto them, Be fruitful, and multiply. (Gen. 1:20–28 KJV)

You can't improve on this familiar story from Genesis, but somehow it had a new meaning for me when I read it on deck this morning. I have more than my share of quiet times at Arbreux,[8] but even there the noise and bustle of civilization intrudes—the sound of a gunshot in the distant woods, a passing car or truck on the road, a dog barking, or human voices at distant houses. Here in the middle

8. Arbreux, "*fr. A Wooded Place,* the name of my home - seven acres in the Shenandoah Valley.

of the Pacific Ocean there is no television, no telephone to ring, not even any sounds of short-wave radio as mine is inoperable. You are compelled here to quietness; only the muffled drone of the ship's diesel engine can be heard.

The sound of silence is something I believe is desperately needed in our world. People need a place and time to be still and meditate on the greatness of creation, to ponder their Maker's caring love for them, to search for resources of wisdom and meaning for living, and to discover anew or for the first time that God is still in charge of the universe. Such a time and place is needed as much for youth as for people in their middle years and beyond. Robin Lee Graham discovered this at the age of twenty-one after traveling 30,600 nautical miles around the world in five years. On the final day of his voyage he summed up some of the lessons he had learned:

> I'd learned so many things at sea—like kindness has got nothing to do with money, and happiness has got nothing to do with rank or race . . . At sea I had learned how little a person needs, not how much. . . . It seemed to me that so many people hold back from doing the things they really want to do because of fear . . . Being alone had made me realize that man is pretty insignificant in the universe, like a speck of dust.[9]

I believe I know what Graham was trying to say about loneliness, though I cannot agree that loneliness and human significance should be linked. Having been created in the image of God, given dominion over all other creatures, and having the potential of being joint-heirs with Christ gives human beings immense significance. However, there

9. Robin Lee Graham, *Dove*. New York: Bantam Books, 1972, pp 180–181. Used by permission.

are people whose self-inflicted loneliness comes from deliberate separation of themselves from others, either because they choose to live as recluses or because their unsavory treatment of other people has alienated them into a loneliness that deprives them of happiness.

Jean-Paul Sartre, French philosopher and founder of existentialism, once wrote: "Hell is other people." I believe that just the opposite is true: hell is being totally alone. Sartre may have meant that other people got in his way or made too many demands on him. Other people may complicate our lives, but without them life becomes unbearably desolate.

Finally, some loneliness is brought about by circumstances beyond our choosing. Such are the vagaries of war, illness, and death that deprive us of lifelong companions or make us refugees from home, wherever home may be. Even then, we are admonished to reach out to others as a means of overcoming our grief and loneliness because all humanity shares these common experiences and all need the warm hand of compassion and caring.

For my part, I know that this voyage is only a temporary separation from friends. Moreover, I'm trying to make new friends with the crew of the ship. I enjoy their fellowship at meals, but this is a working ship and I stay out of their way just as I would not bother a bus driver or an airline pilot. Too, I know that in a short while I will be restored to my friends and family at home, Lord willing. But for the time being, I am finding fellowship with other minds via the good books I'm reading. And I'm keeping a spiritual vigil with friends at home and a host of friends, my extended family, around the world.

August 31, 1999

> By the word of the Lord were the heavens made, their starry host by the breath of His mouth. He gathers the waters of the sea in jars; He puts the deep into storehouses. (Ps. 33:7)

The celestial canopy here over the Pacific is not obscured by artificial light and air pollution. From the bridge deck on clear nights, and minus any cloudiness, you can see all of the stars in the northern hemisphere. These clear night skies over the Pacific enable me to ponder the heavens and view the constellations. Last night I tried to find the big dipper, but some clouds obscured my vision. Nevertheless, I've been reading about the planets, the stars, and constellations in my Audubon guide. Bootes with its bright star Arcturas has always intrigued me. Arcturus, the fourth brightest star in the night sky, is easily found by first finding the Big Dipper then following the curving handle to the next bright star (e.g., to the left when the dipper is "holding water").

Bootes, like all the other constellations, is associated with many legends derived from Greek and Roman mythology. One legend says Bootes was the son of Demeter (Roman, Ceres), the goddess of agriculture, and is credited with inventing the plow. Accordingly, it was placed in the sky to honor an invention of such importance to civilization. In another myth, Bootes was the son of Zeus and his mistress Callisto. Zeus's jealous wife, Hera, transformed Callisto into a bear and sent Bootes out to kill her, but Zeus rescued Callisto and took her into the heavens, where she became Ursa Major, the Great Bear. Arcturus, the principle star seen in the tale of Boote's kite (or the bottom point of the ice cream cone), then became her keeper rather than her hunter.

Nearby in the heavens are the Hunting Dogs of the constellation Canes Venatici. Arcturus is depicted as leading the Hunting Dogs and driving the bears of Ursa Major and Ursa Minor around the pole. Arabian starwatchers saw the circumpolar stars (the bears are always in the North sky circling the North Pole) as sheep, with Bootes as the shepherd. The Chinese saw Bootes as the horn of a huge celestial dragon that ruled the sky at springtime.

Modern youth, with their video games, television, and electronic gadgetry, perhaps have lost the imagination of a shepherd boy at the time of Jesus. Watching the stars and the canopy of heaven, and associating them with the stories heard at the family hearth and around campfires, the shepherds saw the great drama of real life played out in the stars and clouds like chariots of fire on stormy nights and ephemeral armies coming to battle from the western horizon.

Many myths and legends are also associated with other constellations. The pagan myths are interesting, but these do not deter me from a sense of awe and wonder. I still marvel at the splendor of the heavenly canopy, and these quiet moments viewing the stars turn my thoughts to the Creator. For one such as I, whose wanderlust seems often an addiction, I wonder if heaven will provide for me carefree travel to other Milky Ways. Reading the biblical record, I have reason to believe that it shall. If this is true, earth's grand adventure will be magnified many times over. I read in Hebrews, though, that even the heavens will perish in God's own timetable. But if heaven is a stationary place, I shall be content simply rejoicing with the saints!

I believe I may be among a very small minority who have an overwhelming feeling of awe and wonder when I look into the star-filled canopy. Planetariums are like cathedrals for me—places of worship. But how much more the heavens on a clear night! Noted British astronomer, professor David Block, has a slide he shows to audiences that he claims is a photograph of one hundred billion stars. He concludes that if we were to count one star per second it would require two thousand five hundred years to count them.

September 1, 1999

> The earth is the Lord's and everything in it, the world and all who live in it. For he founded it upon the seas and established it upon the waters. (Ps. 24:1)

We awoke this morning to good weather again, though the clouds are a little grayer and there are more scattered about. Captain Mahnke told me yesterday that he gets weather reports from Germany, makes a decision about any changes en route, sends his suggested plan to his company, and they report back "OK." This procedure is required in case of any typhoons or cyclones floating around the Pacific. We went through some rain showers last night because I see dampness on the reefers just below my cabin window.

This morning I walked to the bow (forecastle) of the ship, from which point I have an almost circular view of the ocean horizon. Captain Mahnke informed me that I would most likely see flying fish at the bow. I saw no flying fish today. The ship approached what at first appeared to be a small cloud. The cloud grew larger as we neared, then I saw that it was raining to the South and North. Not until we were well under the cloud did it begin to rain on the ship; the wind grew blustery, and I scurried to cover. Then I saw a rainbow, too, and thought it fortuitous because just last night I had read the account of Noah and the flood and God's promise, when He put His rainbow in the sky, that the earth would never again be totally covered with water.

September 2, 1993

> The purposes of a man's heart are deep waters, but a man of understanding draws them out. (Prov. 20:5)

Captain Mahnke reminded us this morning at breakfast that tomorrow we will cross the International Date Line and set our clocks forward to September 4, thus skipping Friday altogether. However, we make this time up one hour at a time each morning by setting our watches back one hour. So even though it is a "lost" day on the calendar, the universal clock has not changed. The sun still rises and sets on schedule everywhere around the globe just as it always has done for thousands of years. The moon still makes its orbital rotation around the earth with precision. "God is in His heaven, and all is right with the world."

In about three days now we will approach the North China Sea. According to Rachel Carson, one of the deepest places in the world's oceans is just off the coast of the Philippines. Here, too, are mountains which, could we view them from the ocean floor, would be as high and spectacular as the Swiss Alps.

As oceanographers learn more and more about what is beneath the surface, the question occurs again and again: can the submerged masses of the undersea mountains be linked with the famed "lost continents"? Best known is

Atlantis, which according to Plato was a large continent beyond the Pillars of Hercules (Gibraltar). According to Plato's legend, Atlantis was the home of a warlike people ruled by powerful kings who made frequent attacks on the mainland of Europe and Africa, roamed the Mediterranean coast of Europe, and finally attacked Athens. In a single day, however, the island that was Atlantis was obliterated with great earthquakes and volcanic eruptions, and disappeared beneath the sea. Plato wrote that since that time, seagoing vessels could not navigate those waters because of dangerous hidden shoals beneath the surface that could wreck ships. We now know the Atlantic is navigable, but soundings of the ocean's floor prove the existence of what was once a large island now known to be a part of the undersea Atlantic Ridge.

Sailing near the volcanic islands of the Pacific brings some sobering reminders for oceanographers and seismologists. South of Singapore, and perhaps not more than 700 miles off the course by which the Cho Yang Atlas will sail en route to the Suez, is the Sunda Strait. You can find it on the map, adjacent to Java and Sumatra. Rachel Carson records that the greatest explosion of historic time occurred there on August 27, 1883 when the island of Krakatoa was virtually eviscerated. In the spring of 1883, smoke and steam began to escape from the fissures of a volcanic cone on the island, with warnings and hissings as the ground became noticeably warm. In a violent series of eruptions lasting two days, the whole northern half of the cone blew away. The sound of the explosions was heard in the Philippine Islands, in Australia, and on the island of Madagascar, nearly 3,000 miles away. A hundred-foot tsunami (tidal wave) wiped out villages along the Strait and killed tens of thousands.

These recorded events about the mysteries of "the sea around us" add intrigue and interest to the voyage. Add to this the news the First Mate just received on his short wave radio that a massive earthquake has hit Athens. Consider, then, these lines from Psalm 46:1–3:

> God is our refuge and strength, an ever-present help in trouble. Therefore we will not fear, though the earth give way and the mountains fall into the heart of the sea, though its waters roar and foam and the mountains quake with their surging. Selah.

Today I witnessed something seasoned sailors have always known about—flying fish! Many have told how flying fish have landed on the deck of their yacht or small vessel. Seeing them sail over the water was the highlight of my day. For three days I have looked for them without success; today I saw them in multitudes. What surprised me was how far they actually fly. Some sailed for a hundred yards or more, their fins substituting for feathers.

S. C. Brooks wrote of seeing them North of the Marquesas:

> Flying fish . . . are breaking the water every few seconds, and bewitch the beholder by their myriad sizes, shapes, and antics, and their bewildering patterns and shades of deep brown, opal blue, yellow and purple.[10]

Perhaps nowhere other than the Pacific can one sense how vast is earth's encircling sea. We have been sailing now for six days and have seen not a jot of land. And we are destined to go for five more days in like manner. It is easy to understand why the ancient Greeks thought of the ocean

10. From *The Condor,* Vol. 36, No. 5, Sep-Oct. 1934, pp186–187.

as boundless and infinite. Their legends speak of the ocean as an endless stream that flowed forever around the border of the world. Anyone who ventured far out upon it would pass through gathering darkness and come at last to the blending of sea and sky, a place where whirlpools and yawning abysses would draw the traveler down into a dark world from which there was no return. To the Greeks, the sea was their own Mediterranean. Outside, encircling the land world was Oceanus. There in its vast expanse was the home of the gods and of departed spirits. Even now, the darkness of antiquity still lingers over the surface of the waters of our planet. Consider the legend of the Loch Ness monster and the tales one reads about the shipwrecks in the Bermuda triangle.

September 4, 1999

> . . . things that are too amazing for me—the way of a ship on the high seas. (Prov. 30:18–19)

> And so we know and rely on the love God has for us. God is Love. Whoever lives in love lives in God, and God in him. (1 John 14:16)

How nice that we can sleep an hour later each day as we make our way across the Pacific (in my case to awake early and read). We are setting our watches back one hour each day, traveling through approximately one time zone each 24 hours. I was up early this morning and did my exercises including leg splits against the wall, push-ups and crunches (ugh!). (My friend Bill would be pleased.)

Good weather again this morning and the sea is calm with no whitecaps whatsoever. Light cumulous and serous clouds overhead and only faint clouds on the distant horizon to the North. No word of any cyclones or typhoons in the Pacific. That is reassuring, especially at this time of year.

Mentally, I'm in three parts of the world at once. I'm here in the mid-Pacific slowly plodding toward Asia from the East. I'm at home in spirit with family and friends. And I'm in Mongolia plodding toward China from the West via Paul Theroux's book *Riding the Iron Rooster*. I read the book shortly after it was published in 1989 when I was still with the Peace Corps. But it is enlightening to read it again now. After all, I will be setting foot again in China (Hong Kong) in just a few days. Hong Kong was still flying the Union Jack when I was there in May two years ago. Now it is fully a part of China.

The Boson is an important man aboard ship. His responsibility is to keep the ship seaworthy in every respect. Though only two years in service, the Cho Yang Atlas already has scattered rust spots, the result of relentless invasion of salt and seawater. While we are at sea, Boson Tamaeu Tauro and his crew are priming the port side of the main deck of the ship for later painting. He told me this morning that it will be the first time the deck will have been painted since it went into service. The men use electric drill brushes to remove rust and old paint. This obviously is very hard work. Because of the lead, they keep their heads and faces covered with cloths and use breathing masks. The effect is to make them appear like Arab sheiks.

He and his Kiribati crew are always busy; I see them at work even before breakfast. In port their duties entail securing the containers, carrying out docking and undocking maneuvers, and stowing all equipment. Obviously the work ethic has been well instilled in these Kiribati sailors. They have warm smiles and make me feel welcome on board—their home away from home. Their contracts are sometimes for two years' duration, after which they may take home leave. Kiribatis speak English because it was mandated in this British colony, although at home they speak their own language.

There is a definitive "pecking order" of rank aboard ship. In addition to the separate officers' mess, cabins aboard are stratified with the Captain and Chief Engineer on F deck, Chief Officer and 2nd Engineer on E deck, the Cook and Electrician on D deck (where I have the largest cabin with adjacent swimming pool and sauna), the Boson, 3rd Engineer and 3rd Officer on C deck, and all the rest of the crew on A and B decks. The mess and cook's gallery is on A deck. Here, like almost everywhere, the old axiom we learned in military basic training fits: "Rank has its privileges."

In the early mornings I can look outward and upward from my forward cabin windows and see the moon. A week ago it was a full moon; now it is a thin crescent of a quarter moon. It is propitious for me to brood about the moon at this moment in time. Why? Some geophysicists speculate that today there is a great scar on the surface of the globe and that the scar, or depression, holds the Pacific Ocean. According to them, the floor of the Pacific is composed of basalt, the substance of the earth's middle layer, while all of the other oceans are floored with granite, which makes up most of the earth's outer layer. What happened to the Pacific Ocean's granite? The most convenient assumption is that it was torn away when the moon was formed. No one, of course, really knows, but this is the most plausible theory.

September 5, 1999

> The Lord will keep you from all harm; He will watch over your life. The Lord will watch over your coming and going both now and forevermore. (Ps. 121:7–8)

I copied onto diskettes some sermons from the World Wide Web so as to have my devotions on Sundays out here on the high seas. I was up early this morning to read them and so I share the following quote from a sermon by Rev. David Feddes preaching for *The Back to God Hour* as superb food for thought.

> We live in one great universe which is designed, created, and operated by one great God. Every new discovery should impress us even more with the power and divine nature of God. The only fitting response is to glorify Him and give Him thanks. We must adore and worship the Lord who gives us a glimpse of His splendor and wisdom in the things He has made. And we must acknowledge that everything we have comes from Him. Every breath we take, everything we have, is a gift from the hand of God. We owe Him everything, and so we should be grateful to Him. We can't simply believe that there is a God out there, and leave it at that. We must glorify Him as God and give Him thanks."[11]

Another smooth glassy sea and clear skies this morning. Not a speck of land or another vessel on the horizon. The crew tells me we will begin to see more ships as we near Taiwan when we enter the Asian North-South shipping lanes. Also the Captain said that a typhoon was nearing Hong Kong but that it should we dissipated by the time we get there six days hence. I keep looking for some sign of islands because I believe we are nearing the Volcano Islands on my starboard side. One plus for sea travel is that it concentrates the mind sharply on geography; it is reassuring to know just exactly where you are on the planet.

11. From a sermon by Rev. David Feddes, "Educated Fools". Used by permission of Rev. Feddes.

One realization of having spent so many days crossing the Pacific is that there is even more of this same ocean South of the equator in the southern hemisphere. It puts to rest any pygmy thoughts about the waters that cover the earth. Add to this the knowledge gleaned from Rachel Carson's *The Sea Around Us* and one's whole comprehension of the mystery of creation is transformed.

Today the ocean that appears to be so placid is rather forcefully on the move, with powerful forces at work. Currents on the surface and in the deep ocean are constantly on the move, affected by the rotation of the earth, the tidal affects of the moon, the seasonal tilting of the earth, and surface climatic conditions caused by the very movement of the seas. Currents in the deep ocean move to the surface with cooler temperatures, powered partly by the heated surface waters of the tropics. Thus, the phenomena of El Niño, La Niña, tropical storms, hurricanes, and cyclones determine weather conditions on the continents, emanating in large part from the Pacific. That's a simplistic explanation of a very complex and baffling enigma. Scientists of all sorts work at solving the "problems." Pondering the wonder of it all, I am content to leave it all in the hands of the Creator.

Late afternoons paint sunsets too magnificent to describe. I can view them from my cabin's forward windows as we head due West toward the setting sun. Tonight I think of myself as the benefactor of a very private, albeit ephemeral, Winslow Homer. Scattered over an infinite horizon are rainstorms and rainbows with beams of sunlight penetrating thunderheads in the western sky. Sailors for centuries have been treated to these original seascape masterpieces painted on the widest canvas known to mankind. Red sky at night, sailors' delight!

Ravi Zacharias wrote that "Oscar Wilde once said that we do not appreciate sunsets because we do not have to pay for them. Oscar Wilde was wrong. We can 'pay' for sunsets by living in accordance with the purpose of our Creator and of His grand design."[12]

September 6, 1999

> The heavens declare the glory of God; the skies proclaim the work of His hands. . . . In the heavens He has pitched a tent for the sun. . . . It rises at one end of the heavens and makes its circuit to the other. (Ps. 19:1, 4, 6)

I awoke in the middle of the night and heard rain whipping my cabin's forward windows. The sky is filled with thunderheads this morning and some to the South appear ominous. The wonder is that we have gone eight days now without any bad weather of any sort. Never mind the portentous clouds because the ocean itself is calm and free of whitecaps. The ship plods on in a gentle rolling motion.

It plods on toward Taiwan and China. Eventually, no doubt, hostilities will break out between these two Chinese places. (Please, not while I'm stopping by.) The uneasy truce that has kept them neutralized all these years is something of a miracle. I read that Taiwan still uses Hong Kong as its entrepot to the mother country. In fact, it is very likely that this German ship will be picking up goods in Kaohsiung that will be offloaded in Hong Kong, with final destination to such places as Beijing and Canton. Hong Kong has always been the freest of free ports. It is too early to tell if it will remain that way under communist supervision.

12. Ravi Zacharias, *Can Man Live Without God?*. Dallas: Word Incorporated, 1995, p. 160. Used by permission.

Hong Kong conjures up all sorts of images as I remember my three previous visits there. I keep going back to Jan Morris's superb word pictures:

> . . . Hong Kong is astonishingly beautiful. It is made so partly by its setting, land and sea so exquisitely interacting, but chiefly by its impression of irresistible activity. It is like a caldron, seething, hissing, hooting, arguing, enmeshed in a labyrinth of tunnels and overpasses, with those skyscrapers erupting everywhere into view, with ferries churning and hovercraft splashing and great jets flying in, with fleets of ships lying always offshore, with double-decker buses and clanging tramcars, with a car it seems for every square foot of roadway, with a pedestrian for every square inch of sidewalk, and funicular trains crawling up and down the mountainside, and small scrubbed-faced policemen scudding about on motorbikes—all in all, with a pace of life so unremitting, a sense of movement and enterprise so challenging, that one's senses are overwhelmed by the sheer glory of human animation.[13]

As we draw nearer to Hong Kong and I read more books from the passengers' library about the place, I am reminded of its Chineseness and the glut of religions in this perhaps most exotic city on earth. Since my first visit in 1969, I have had an insatiable interest in every magazine or newspaper article about the place. Because the city has become the repository of refugees from all parts of the world, some religious rites of one sort or another are going on all the time. The Chinese of Hong Kong believe in gods and ghosts, signs and auguries, and all sorts of supernatural faiths and superstitions. Feng Shui is only one of the manifestations of this pantheon. Small mirrors hang outside

13. Jan Morris, *Hong Kong*. New York: First Vintage Books, 1989, p.155. Used by permission of Random House, Inc.

houses and shops for warding off evil spirits. There are private shrines to kitchen gods, joss sticks for divining the future or making a life decision, cabalistic papers to be pulled out of a bag to divine good luck, and assorted stones, strips of red paper, ribbons, and candle stumps to mark the holy sites of animism. In 1980 seventy-eight distinct divinities were honored at a single festival in the Hong Kong New Territories village of Fanling.

With their pantheon of gods, the Chinese are forever celebrating some effervescent festival. Flotillas of miniature ships with lighted candles are launched into the sea (I saw this festival underway once in Bangkok, too); long dragon trains wind their way through the shopping districts and alleys; the full moon is honored with family outings and picnics on any high hill where they can find space; the spirits of the dead are communed with over five course meals in cemeteries; wild dragon-boat races are rowed; and Chinese New Year takes on a Mardi-Gras atmosphere with parades, illegal fireworks, reveling, eating, and drinking.

Half a million Chinese are either Muslims or Christians, but many more are Daoists, Buddhists, or animists. Some pay homage to an eclectic, layered combination of religions and gods; the gods are not so much worshiped as entreated for favors. Their innumerable gods include monkey gods, earth and sea gods, hearth gods, water gods, martial gods, gods of happiness, mercy, affluence, justice, long life, wisdom, wealth, aptitude, and more. One of the reported hazards of driving in Hong Kong was the belief among elderly Chinese that if they stood close enough to a passing car any evil spirits at their heels would be run over. Is it any wonder that I find Hong Kong such an immensely interesting place to visit?

Over against these reminders of the Chinese assortment of gods my thoughts turn once more to the apostle John's letters written at the end of his long life. Summing up his belief in just three words, the great saint who stood by the mother of Jesus as He hung on the cross, the one apostle who stayed near Him until His death, wrote:

> God is love . . . And so we know and rely on the love God has for us . . . Whoever lives in love lives in God, and God in him. In this way, love is made complete among us so that we will have confidence on the day of judgment, because in this world we are like Him . . . We love, because He first loved us. (1 John 4:16, 19)

Last evening, the lyrics and melody of my favorite hymn kept running through my thoughts like a benediction:

> O Let the love of God enfold you
> With His Spirit and His love
> Let Him fill your heart and satisfy your soul.
> O Let Him have the things that hold you
> And His Spirit like a dove
> Will descend upon your life and make you whole.
>
> O come and sing this song with gladness
> As your hearts are filled with joy.
> Lift your hands in sweet surrender to His name.
> O give him all your tears and sadness
> Give Him all your years of pain,
> And you'll enter into life in Jesus name.
>
> Jesus, O Jesus, come and fill your lambs.
> Jesus, O Jesus, come and fill your lambs.

Those lyrics have returned to me at times when I needed most to sense the presence of the Holy Spirit in my life. These long days at sea provide time to think about where

I've been and where I'm going spiritually with my life, to reconsider what has greatest meaning for me, and to assess whether I'm making the most of the days vouchsafed me. Harold Kushner made this provocative observation:

> I believe that it is not dying that people are afraid of. Something else, something more unsettling and more tragic than dying frightens us. We are afraid of never having lived, of coming to the end of our days with the sense that we were never really alive, that we never figured out what life was for.[14]

Meaning for my days and for my life? I found meaning when Christ found me. For whatever I do with the time yet allotted me, I would hope and pray that my life would testify to the great joy of the Christian life. I would willingly testify, but the testimony need not be forced or contrived, for it is not in my providence to attempt to arrange the salvation of another soul. I believe the Christian life means allowing God to love others through me while I wait patiently upon Him. John Milton, in his poem *Requiem* expressed my sentiments better:

> When I consider how my light is spent
> Ere half my days, in this dark world and wide,
> And that one talent which is death to hide
> Lodged with me useless, though my soul
> More bent
>
> To serve therewith my Maker, and present
> My true account, lest He returning chide,—
> Doth God exact day-labour, light denied?
> I fondly ask:—But Patience, to prevent

14. Harold Kushner, *When All You've Ever Wanted Isn't Enough.* New York: Pocket Books (Simon and Schuster), 1985, p. 156. Used by permission.

> That murmur, soon replies; God doth not need
> Either man's work, or His own gifts: who best
> Bear His mild yoke, they serve Him best: His state
> Is kingly; thousands at His bidding speed
> And post o'er land and ocean without rest:—
> They also serve who only stand and wait.

September 7, 1999

> The voice of the Lord is over the waters; the God of glory thunders. The Lord thunders over the mighty waters. (Ps. 29:3)

Yesterday we passed through a storm and there was indeed thunder and lightning. I went up on the bridge and asked the third mate whether it was safe to use the swimming pool while the ship was passing through a storm with lightning. "No problem," he said. The ship is equipped to neutralize lightning. Also, the ship won't lose power during a storm because all electricity depends totally on the diesel engines.

We passed the Volcano Islands this morning at about 0400, according to Captain Mahnke. That means we've already begun the slow descent to lower latitude into the North China Sea. Soon we should be seeing more ocean traffic. Once we reach Taiwan, the second mate says, we will be in sight of land somewhere all the way to Felixstowe. We will be passing through the South China Sea en route to Singapore, then through the rather narrow Strait of Mallaca into the Andaman Sea, then westward again through the Indian Ocean to the Arabian Sea, the Gulf of Aden, and into the Red Sea. Sometime late today or tomorrow we will cross the Tropic of Cancer. If this voyage does nothing else, it will reacquaint me with my geography of the world.

This morning promises to be another day of smooth sailing. There are cumulous clouds about, but the sea is calm again—extraordinarily good weather at sea for this time of the year, according to the Captain, and of course, he ordered it just for me!

Our cook is Filipino and he has an excellent repertoire of international recipes. The soups are especially delicious. For breakfast I have Swiss musli (their spelling) every morning, sometimes supplemented by eggs, an egg roll, or pancakes. We have soup for lunch every day, followed by the principal entrée of the day—beef, pork, chicken, duck (once), turkey, or fish. These are supplemented with either rice or potatoes and a variety of vegetables. Thursdays on German ships are "Sailors' Sundays," meaning that the noon meal is either steak or turkey. Steak, turkey, or duck are also served on Sundays. And on both Thursday and Sunday we also have ice cream. The evening meal is usually a smorgasbord of cheeses, lunchmeats, fruits and vegetables that we choose by serving ourselves. There's no fear of being undernourished, so I am making good use of the pool, gym, and sauna.

The pool is filled with seawater pumped in from the ocean. It is briny, but doesn't smell of fish. And of course, it is marvelously buoyant. So far they've changed the water three times, and each time it's a few degrees warmer. Today I was in the pool three times to relieve the tropical stickiness after hiking on the main deck.

I am now reading Peter Mayle's *A Year In Provence*, found in the ship's library. Also Pico Iyer's *Falling Off the Map*. Both are excellent travel memoirs.

September 8, 1999

Once more a blue sky and a placid sea greeted us this morning as we tread this last full day across the Pacific toward Kaohsiung. We are due to dock there tomorrow at noon. I look at the map and see that I am half way around the world. This is no big deal for the crew, however. They go back and forth from the United States to Asia and Europe like the pendulum on a clock. I'm certain that if they were paid mileage, they would all be wealthy.

Captain Mahnke told me at dinner last night that he had seen some whales yesterday. I will keep a watch for them today. The eyes play tricks on you when you are watching the ocean endlessly for any signs of life. Did I see a shark yesterday? Or did I see an ocean tuna? Was that a giant sea turtle? I cannot be certain . . . but just maybe they were all there. I did see many more flying fish, some of which were right outside my window on the starboard side of the ship.

My laptop computer sits atop a desk directly facing the cabin window, and this morning as we draw nearer to Taiwan I see that clouds have thickened above this Pacific sea of vibrant colors—indigo and aqua and milky emerald, splattered now with whitecapped waves. Dramatic thunderheads pierce high into the sapphire sky—ephemeral mountains of bright, white steam with foothills painted shades of mauve and ginger and dusky rose. A milky stream like laundry suds as far as the eye can see follows in our wake, generated by the ship's powerful rudders in these briny waters. In all of this time and distance, not once have I seen a jet aircraft's vapor trail in the sky. The thought comes to mind that these common multicolored scenes of water and sky alternated with each night's canopy of planets and stars are the career sailor's world for the greater part of his life.

Yet even this isn't all, for the sailor's world scenes change with the seasons. Rachel Carson has written movingly about the changing face of the sea:

> For the sea as a whole, the alternation of day and night, the passage of the seasons, the procession of the years, are lost in its vastness, obliterated in its own changeless eternity. But the surface waters are different. The face of the sea is always changing. Crossed by colors, lights, and moving shadows, sparkling in the sun, mysterious in the twilight, its aspects and its moods vary hour by hour. The surface waters move with the tides, stir to the breath of the winds, and rise and fall to the endless, hurrying forms of the waves. Most of all, they change with the advance of the seasons.[15]

Carson explains how each season has its effect on the surface of the oceans. Spring brings diatoms and microscopic plants of plankton, turning vast areas of the sea red or brown or green. The summer sea may glitter with millions of pinpricks of light caused by phosphorescent shrimp like an immense swarm of fireflies. Autumn brings fall flowering of the flagellates, producing a fresh blaze of phosphorescence, making the wave crests appear to be aflame. "Man, in his vanity," she writes, "subconsciously attributes a human origin of any light not of moon or stars or sun. Lights on the shore, lights moving over the water, mean lights kindled and controlled by other men, serving purposes understandable to the human mind. Yet here are lights that flash and fade away, lights that come and go for reasons meaningless to man."[16]

And sailors in the great circle routes of the high seas have yet added diversity: endless days if ships ply the Arctic or Antarctic regions in summer; all that ice to both

15. Rachel Carson, *The Sea Around Us*. New York: The New American Library, 1961., p.41. Used by permission.

16. Ibid., p.45.

be dazzled by and to avoid (the Titanic taught wise sailors that lesson); endless nights in winter; the aurora borealis to bewitch the bridge watch; and rainbows in the midnight sun sans sunsets.

Late summer begins the migration of the phalaropes, small brown birds, wheeling and turning, rising and dipping their way South from the plankton meadows of the Arctic. The phalaropes nest on the Arctic tundra, rear their young, and then begin their slow southward journey over open water, eventually crossing the equator. I first saw them with binoculars from the bow of the ship when we were just four days West of San Francisco. I thought they appeared to be traveling solo, but noticed later that usually there would be two or three to follow. What amazes is their stamina to remain airborne those thousands of miles, spiritual cousins of the hummingbird and monarch butterfly, following instincts ages old. But even the most avid ornithologists are denied viewing them in migration except on a voyage such as mine.

Only moments ago I saw a seagull making its way directly toward our ship. I believe it may at this moment be perched on one of the containers. It's a reminder of Noah's dove sent out to find dry land! I've seen rainbows all along the way.

I am reading Anne Morrow Lindbergh's *Gift from the Sea.*

> Modern communication loads us with more problems than the human frame can carry. It is good for our hearts, our minds, our imaginations to be stretched; but body, nerve, endurance, and life-span are not so elastic. My heart cannot implement in action the demands of all the people to whom my heart responds.[17]

17. Anne Morrow Lindbergh, *Gift from the Sea.* New York: Signet Books, 1957. p.122. Used by permission.

Nor do I believe are we so required. I believe the Scriptures teach that salvation is purely and simply a gift of grace. His burden is light when we take up His yoke. We cannot earn our way into heaven with good deeds; nor should our primary motive be to earn favor with man or God. That is what the Pharisees tried: doing and keeping the law. Jesus simply commanded, "Thou shalt love." Therefore, I can simplify my life by choosing to love, recognizing that I cannot take upon my shoulders the burdens of all mankind. I can wait upon Him, and He will show me what I can do with my limited resources and energies. Life is so much simpler His way.

Landfall In Asia

September 9, 1999—Kaohsiung, Taiwan

> . . . for in that voyage from which no man returns Landfall and Departure are instantaneous, merging together into one moment of supreme and final attention.
>
> *The Mirror of the Sea*
>
> —Joseph Conrad

Landfall! The southern end of Taiwan, this land once called Formosa, is just ahead of us this morning. We will dock in Kaohsiung by noon. I was in Taipei in 1969 on leave from Japan en route to Hong Kong. I remember coming in winter and everything here was lush and green. I had forgotten how mountainous is this island. Oh, it is exhilarating to see Land after eleven days of nothing but horizon!

Joseph Conrad in his classic book *The Mirror of the Sea* writes that every sailor's goal is a Landfall (capitalized because of its importance in the mariner's mind). Landfall for sailors is the first sight of land after being at sea, not the arrival on shore or in port. A departure is not the pulling away from port but rather the last visible sight of land as the ship heads out to sea.

Now there are many small fishing boats, tugboats, ferries, tankers, and other freighters in the Taiwan Strait as we head northward to the port. Hans Werner, the Chief Officer (First Mate) told me that we will see many ships now all the way to Singapore as we head down the China coast tomorrow to Hong Kong, thence to Singapore and Malaysia with Vietnam and Saigon on the starboard side.

Today in the harbor I've watched many ships go by: the Greta Maersk, Aviero, UniGlory—Panama, World Hampton-Monrovia, Venus, APL Pearl—Singapore, Timor—Jakarta, MV UniConcert—Keelung, BDW Leopard—Bergen, China Steel Investor—Kaohsiung, American President Lines' President Truman, a containerliner, and others. Not many ships have honorary names of people. Someone could do an interesting dissertation on the naming of ships.

The bulletin board on our Deck A says that we sail at 0500 tomorrow morning. Next stop—Hong Kong!

> Over the centuries, with all the skill and ingenuity and reasoning powers of his mind, man has sought to explore and investigate even its most remote parts, so that he might re-enter it mentally and imaginatively. He cannot control or change the ocean as, in his brief tenancy of earth, he has subdued and plundered the continents. In the artificial world of his cities and towns, he forgets the true nature of his planet and the long vistas of history, in which the existence of the race of men has occupied a mere moment in time. The sense of all these things comes to him most clearly in the course of a long ocean voyage, when he watches day after day the receding rim of the horizon, ridged and furrowed by waves; when at

night he becomes aware of the earth's rotation as the stars pass overhead; or when, alone in this world of water and sky, he feels the loneliness of his earth in space. And then, as never on land, he knows the truth that his world is a water world, a planet dominated by its covering mantel of ocean, in which the continents are but transient intrusions of land above the surface of the all encircling sea.

The Sea Around Us
—Rachel Carson

September 10, 1999

We pulled away from the Kaohsiung dock at 0700 and are now headed due West for China and Hong Kong. As expected, I've seen a number of freighters and fishing trawlers along the way. I counted more than sixty vessels on the horizon at one time this afternoon then quit counting. Most of them are fishing trawlers, some of which passed nearby. It is heartening to have fellow travelers after going so long without an entourage.

Before we left Kaohsiung this morning, I was reminded of the thousands of refugees I had seen in Hong Kong in 1969, many of whom were living on boats at Wan Chi. Two Chinese sampans passed the Cho Yang Atlas, loaded for the most part with the familiar nondescript tied-up bundles. On the back of each vessel was an old woman, looking wistfully out to sea. One of them wore a simple gray smock and an expression of great sadness. Somewhere, long ago and deep in China, I suspected, she had left friends and family during one of the many upheavals, fleeing to what was then Formosa as a refugee. It is the sad story of all the old people who survive in modern Taiwan. Perhaps on this junk she was making her way back to Hong Kong to be reunited with long separated loved ones. I hoped so, but I doubted it.

We are crossing what is the northernmost part of the South China Sea. From the large number of fishing trawlers, these waters are obviously a productive breeding ground for fish, and must be the source of a vast quantity of food for not only China, but for much of Asia. Our steward told me at lunch today that sailors always catch lots of fish when their ship is docked in Hong Kong—just throw a line overboard!

September 11, 1999—Hong Kong

We arrived in Hong Kong early this morning at 0130. The one event of this voyage that I anticipated with great excitement was our arrival in Hong Kong. On each of my three previous visits to Hong Kong, I imagined the excitement of arriving by ship.[18] Had I not cruised the harbor so many times on the Star Ferry? I had also toured the harbor on a Chinese junk and taken the ferry over to Lantau Island. Yet I knew it would be a uniquely exciting experience to actually arrive in Hong Kong by ship. Careful what you wish for. Jan Morris described the parade of freighters in Hong Kong harbor in her epic tableau, Hong Kong:

> The ships are still coming. One after the other they loom out of the West Lamma Channel. In the distance they look no more than shimmery hulks, shapeless and intangible, but slowly they resolve themselves, as they pass Lamma on the starboard side, Cheung Chau on the port, into the huge ungainly forms of container vessels, like floating warehouses, their decks piled so high with gray boxes that their bridges are almost hidden. . . . It is the

18. My impressions of Hong Kong also appear in my book *Pondering My Passage*: Baltimore: American Literary Press, 1995.

> only deepwater harbor between Singapore and Shanghai, and is by common consent one of the most spectacular sights on earth.[19]

Today has been a trip down memory lane. I left the ship this morning at 0730, just an hour after we had docked. I wanted to return to the legendary Star Ferry and make that trip across the harbor one more time—and I did. Regrettably, I didn't have time to take the Peak Tram to the top as I've always done before. I went back to the Salisbury YMCA to buy postcards and books and to the Peninsula Hotel, but due to lack of time didn't get to have tea in the lobby as I've done before. The Peninsula is the grand dame of all the five star hotels in the world. Once it had the most fabulous view in the world, but no longer. The Hong Kong Culture Center and other buildings now obstruct the view across the bay to Hong Kong Island and Victoria. I went to the Mandarin Oriental Hotel, the Peninsula's other five-star rival and had lunch—a Veggie Burger—in the Café.

I strolled through the Ocean Terminal again and marveled at how high the prices are now. When I was in Hong Kong in 1969, the standard phrase used by Americans was "you will go broke saving money in Hong Kong" because people flocked there to have clothes tailor-made, and bragged that they saved enough by shopping to pay their airfare and hotel bill. Such "savings" no longer exist in Hong Kong. Prices now equate to upscale shopping mall prices in the United States. However, there are street (black market) vendors, and I bought a navy cashmere sweater for thirteen dollars—labeled Ralph Lauren!

I wanted to get a photo of one of those high-rise apartment buildings adorned with laundry from every balcony;

---

19. Jan Morris, *Hong Kong*. New York: First Vintage Books, 1989, p.33. Used by permission of Random House, Inc.

they still exist, just as colorful and Chinese as ever, but the taxi driver couldn't stop safely on the freeway. I wanted to take a harbor cruise again on a red Chinese junk complete with sails, but didn't have enough time. I wanted to get a photo of one of the rickshaw drivers, and I did. There were only four rickshaws left at the Star Ferry on the Victoria side, complete with their shirtless drivers; sadly, this is the only place I know where they still exist—an endangered species. My rickshaw man was thrilled to have his picture taken for $3 U.S., and insisted that I get in the rickshaw seat so he could take my picture too. I wanted to send and receive e-mail, and I did so at the Kowloon Hotel's Business Center. I was back at the ship by 1630, because the morning's taxi driver told me that if I waited any later, the traffic jam would be intolerable, and I took him at his word.

When I returned "home" to the Cho Yang Atlas, I had an overwhelming sense of belonging here aboard ship. Why? I suppose it was a relief to be off the crowded sidewalks and free of the constant attack on one's senses—the roar of traffic, the smells both pleasant and unpleasant, too many exotic sights for the human mind to absorb and process. Also at my cabin door I had long letters from John and Rosemary Johnson, friends who live in Bluff, a port town at the very bottom tip of New Zealand's southern most island. What a great joy for me to get mail—anywhere, anytime, but especially when you're ten thousand miles from home.

September 12, 1999

We departed Hong Kong sometime after midnight but, exhausted from the busy day ashore, I slept through the leave-taking. Leaving at night from our berth in upper Kowloon, I knew I would not be able to see the Kowloon-

Victoria waterfront with its dazzling night lights and skyscrapers anyway. Now our route takes us due South into the South China Sea to Singapore. Early tomorrow morning we will be about fifty miles off the coast of Saigon. We are scheduled to arrive in Singapore on Tuesday and depart Wednesday with the next stop Suez, but only to queue for our pass with a convoy of other ships through the Canal.

Psalm 40:5 provides my meditation for this Sunday morning:

> Many, O Lord my God, are the wonders you have done. The things you have done. The things You have planned for us no one can recount to You; were I to speak and tell of them, they would be too many to declare.

I am reading Ravi Zacharias's book, *Can Man Live Without God?* Will Durant once declared the book's title as "the greatest question of our time." The book is best described as an intellectual defense of the Christian faith. I believe that the Christian faith needs no defense any more than God Himself needs to be defended. But this book is nevertheless an excellent apologetic for the Christian worldview and contains a great deal of positive provocative thoughts to ponder. It has particular significance for me at this time out here on the high seas.

"The older you get," writes Zacharias, "the more it takes to fill your heart with wonder, and only God is big enough for that. Not only is He big enough, but in Christian terms He is also near enough." Zacharias writes that this was the discovery of the great mind and genius of poet Francis Thompson, whose most enduring work was the poem *The Hound of Heaven.* As a young man Thompson lived a vagabond life on the streets of London, wandering through two areas of the city. During the day he satisfied his addiction to opium, hanging out with the losers in London's Charing Cross district. At night he would sleep by the banks of the River Thames.

Despite his constant and deliberate running from God, Thompson kept in touch with the Scriptures, and one passage, the story of Jacob, began to haunt him. Jacob, like himself, spent most of his life on the run. Thompson read about Jacob's dream in which he saw a ladder between heaven and earth and the Lord Himself at the top of the ladder. When Jacob awakened from that dream he said, "Surely the Lord is in this place, and I was not aware of it" (Gen. 28:16). As Francis Thompson brooded on this story, his heart must have been filled with wonder and he experienced a dramatic conversion, something akin to the apostle Paul's encounter with Christ on the road to Damascus. Thompson expressed his wonder in this deeply felt poem:

O world invisible, we view thee,
O world intangible, we touch thee,
O world unknowable, we know thee,
Inapprehensible, we clutch thee!

Does the fish soar to find the ocean,
The eagle plunge to find the air—
Do we ask of the stars in motion
If they have rumour of Thee there?

Nor where the wheeling systems darken,
And our benumbed conceiving soars!-
The drift of pinions, would we hearken,
Beats at our own clay-shuttered doors.

The angels keep their ancient places;-
Turn but a stone, and start a wing!

'Tis ye, 'tis your estranged faces,
That miss the many- splendoured thing.

But when so sad thou canst not sadder
Cry—and upon they so sore loss
Shall shine the traffic of Jacob's ladder
Pitched betwixt Heaven and Charing Cross.

Yea, in the night, my Soul, my daughter,
Cry—clinging Heaven by the hems;
And lo, Christ walking on the water
Not of Gennesaret, but Thames![20]

I ponder now these lines again and check my calendar. In just twenty-five days I'll hop on London's "tube" and exit at Leicester Square. Because there I'll be at Charing Cross Road, "book heaven," as I have done before when I've been in this exciting city. (The Charing Cross neighborhood must be a more respectable place now than it was when Thompson lived on its streets.) I'll think of Francis Thompson when I walk the neighborhood and saunter over to the Thames on probably a rainy afternoon. And, Lord willing, my thoughts too will be filled with wonder. A wonder that I'm there again . . . and that I've come all the way around the world in the opposite direction to get there.

The sky has become overcast as we make our way South on the South China Sea. As expected, I've seen several fishing trawlers and at least one freighter, though their distance makes it impossible to tell in which direction they travel. It is just a comforting feeling to have fellow travelers out here on the seas. Unlike all the previous sunsets of this voyage, I will see today's sunset on the starboard side,

20. Francis Thompson, *Complete Poetical Works of Francis Thompson.* New York: Boni and Liveright, 1913, p.356–7).

directly out my cabin window. Heretofore, we were headed due West and the sun was setting in front of the ship.

Also following the ship this afternoon was a giant bird, akin to the albatross, diving in front of the ship for flying fish, a genus of the gannet family.

September 13, 1999—Near Saigon

Another beautiful yet windy day and I am back in my cabin after a long walk on the main deck. The crew is painting the floor of the main deck on the port side now, so I confine my exercise to the forecastle—the top deck of the bow. I follow this with aqua jogging in the pool for about thirty minutes. I do all of my other exercises before breakfast each day.

The Captain says we are scheduled to arrive in Singapore at about 2100 and will sail for the Suez within twenty-four hours. That means a short visit to the Raffles will be possible.

In Singapore I hope to make a nostalgic return to the Raffles Hotel. In 1976 I stayed at this famous British colonial hotel for three days in the same suite where Somerset Maugham had spent several winters and where he is reported to have written *Of Human Bondage*. At that time the hotel's continued operation was in question because of its run-down condition. The guidebooks described it as "tired." There were threadbare drapes and counterpanes, over-worn carpets, and chipped woodwork in the rooms. The plumbing was antique, but it worked. Downstairs, the dining room showed the same signs of age and neglect, but the aging British-trained waiters wore bleached threadbare white towels properly over their arms as they served your linen-covered table set with antique china and silver.

Despite the guidebooks' poor rating, I insisted on staying there because of its legendary past. From the 1930s through the 1950s the Raffles Hotel boasted that it had been host to all the famous people of the world—"everybody who was anybody," so the legends went. I asked for the scrapbooks and was allowed to read about the decadent eighteen-course meals and the people who partook. Now I read that Westin's multi-million dollar renovation has made it again one of the grand hotels of the world. So I look forward to having lunch there and pondering its illustrious history.

The last journey that had taken me full circle around the world was in 1976 when I was dispatched by the American Red Cross to Guam to assist in the aftermath of Typhoon Pamela. I traded in my return airline ticket for passage to Hong Kong, Singapore, Tehran, Tel Aviv, and Paris en route home. I spent a week in Israel, but did not get to Egypt as I had wished. This time I will pass through Egypt, but will not set foot on Egyptian soil.

Egypt—that legendary land that conjures up images of Haji Baba, Aladdin's lamp, gorgeous oriental carpets spread out in sensual souks, mysterious minarets and holy men calling the faithful to prayer, treasure laden burial chambers beneath puzzling pyramids, Pharaohs, Tutankhamen, Anwar Sadat, Omar Sharif as Dr. Zhivago, the story of Moses, and the pivotal historical event of Old Testament times: the Exodus. I have always wanted to go there. Passing through will do. In preparation, I've read and reread the Exodus story several times.

I include the full text here in hopes that the reader will focus on the wonder of it all and sense again the glory of God as I have. Better still, read Exodus from the beginning.

> When Pharaoh let the people go God did not lead them on the road through the Philistine country, though that was shorter. For God said, "If they face war, they might change their minds and return to Egypt." So God led

the people around by the desert road toward the Red Sea. The Israelites went up out of Egypt armed for battle.

Moses took the bones of Joseph with him because Joseph had made the sons of Israel swear an oath. He had said, "God will surely come to your aid, and then you must carry my bones up with you from this place."

After leaving Succoth they camped at Etham on the edge of the desert. By day the Lord went ahead of them in a pillar of cloud to guide them on their way and by night in a pillar of fire to give them light, so that they could travel by day or night. Neither the pillar of cloud by day nor the pillar of fire by night left its place in front of the people.

Then the Lord said to Moses, "Tell the Israelites to turn back and encamp near Pi Hahiroth, between Middol and the sea. They are to encamp by the sea, directly opposite Baal Zephon. Pharaoh will think, 'The Israelites are wandering around in confusion, hemmed in by the desert.'

And I will burden Pharaoh's heart, and he will pursue them. But I will gain glory for Myself through Pharaoh and all his army, and the Egyptians will know that I am the Lord." So the Israelites did this.

When the king of Egypt was told that the people had fled, Pharaoh and his officials changed their minds about them and said, "What have we done? We have let the Israelites go and have lost their services!" So he had his chariot made ready and took his army with him. He took six hundred of the best chariots, along with all the other chariots of Egypt, with officers over all of them. The Lord hardened the heart of Pharaoh king of Egypt, so that he pursued the Israelites, who were marching out boldly. The Egyptians—all Pharaoh's horses and chariots, horsemen and troops—pursued the Israelites and overtook them as they camped by the sea near Pi Hahiroth, opposite Baal Zephon.

As Pharaoh approached, the Israelites looked up, and there were the Egyptians, marching after them. They were terrified and cried out to the Lord. They said to Moses, "Was it because there were no graves in Egypt that you brought us to the desert to die? What have you done to us by bringing us out of Egypt? Didn't we say to you in Egypt, 'Leave us alone; let us serve the Egyptians'? It would have been better for us to serve Egyptians than to die in the desert!"

Moses answered the people, "Do not be afraid. Stand firm and you will see the deliverance the Lord will bring you today. The Egyptians you see today you will never see again. The Lord will fight for you; you need only to be still."

Then the Lord said to Moses, "Why are you crying out to me? Tell the Israelites to move on. Raise your staff and stretch out your hand over the sea to divide the water so that the Israelites can go through the sea on dry ground. I will harden the hearts of the Egyptians so that they will go in after them. And I will gain glory through Pharaoh and all his army, through his chariots and his horsemen. The Egyptians will know that I am the Lord when I gain glory through Pharaoh, his chariots, and horsemen.

Then the angel of God, who had been traveling in front of Israel's army, withdrew and went behind them. The pillar of cloud also moved from in front and stood behind them coming between the armies of Egypt and Israel. Throughout the night the cloud brought darkness to the one side and light to the other side; so neither went near the other all night long.

Then Moses stretched out his hand over the sea, and all the night the Lord drove the sea back with a strong east wind and turned it into dry land. The waters were divided, and the Israelites went through the sea on dry ground, with a wall of water on their right and on their left.

> The Egyptians pursued them, and all Pharaoh's horses and chariots and horsemen followed them into the sea. During the last watch of the night the Lord looked down from the pillar of fire and cloud and threw it into confusion. He made the wheels of their chariots come off so that they had difficulty driving. And the Egyptians said, "Let's get away from the Israelites! The Lord is fighting for them against Egypt."
>
> Then the Lord said to Moses, "Stretch out your hand over the sea so that the waters may flow back over the Egyptians and their chariots and horsemen. Moses stretched out his hand over the sea, and at daybreak the sea went back to its place. The Egyptians were fleeing toward it, and the Lord swept them into the sea. The water flowed back and covered the chariots and horsemen—the entire army of Pharaoh that had followed the Israelites into the sea. Not one of them survived.
>
> But the Israelites went through the sea on dry ground, with a wall of water on their right and on their left. That day the Lord saved Israel from the hands of the Egyptians, and Israel saw the Egyptians lying dead on the shore. And when the Israelites saw the great power the Lord displayed against the Egyptians, the people feared the Lord and put their trust in Him and in Moses His servant. (Ex. 13:17–14:31)

King David, spiritual heir to Moses, would later remember his Hebrew history and write:

> He turned the waters into dry land, they passed through the waters on foot—Come let us rejoice in Him. (Ps. 66:6)

Indeed! Let us rejoice!

September 14, 1999

> O God, our Savior, the hope of all the ends of the earth and of the farthest seas, who formed the mountains by your power . . . who stilled the roaring waves, and the turmoil of the nations. Those living far away fear your wonders, where morning dawns and evening fades. You call forth songs of joy. (Ps. 65:5–8)

I am reading the Psalms now and I'm struck by the many references the Psalmist makes to the sea. The seas he knew were the Red Sea and Mediterranean, whence we are headed. There are references in the Psalms, too, of course, to Mt. Sinai, and if the sky is reasonably clear, I should see Mt. Sinai on the eastern horizon shortly after we enter the Red Sea. I remember flying over it en route to Paris from Yemen in 1991. Our route then took us along the eastern side of the Red Sea and over the troubled city of Beirut before turning due West over Cyprus. A Christian cannot travel anywhere in this part of the world without some reference to the biblical record and history of Israel. Remarkably, much of the region remains unchanged and the ancient descriptions of the land found in the Bible still apply.

We have calm seas and overcast skies this morning, with lots of blue shining through fluffy cumulous clouds tinged with rouge by the early morning sunrise. I remember tropical skies like this in Dar Es Salaam, Tanzania, and it whets my memories of frangipani and bougainvillea in other places near the equator. In Singapore we will be as near to the equator as we will get on this voyage at about six degrees latitude North.

Already this morning we have passed two freighters. One was a petroleum tanker, distinguished by lying low in the water, and the other was a container ship of the Evergreen line. I watch the passing parade of ships with Minolta binoculars I bought in Japan thirty years ago. Binoculars are standard equipment for sailors.

Reading, of course, occupies the greater part of my time aboard ship. I am underlining and transcribing the thoughts and paragraphs that have special value from several sources. I brought aboard a worthy selection of books and found others in the ship's small library. Ravi Zacharias quotes Malcolm Muggeridge's inspiring words on his discovery of a personal relationship with Jesus Christ:

> I may, I suppose, regard myself as a relatively successful man. People occasionally stare at me in the streets. That's fame. I can fairly easily earn enough money to qualify for admission to the higher slopes of the Internal Revenue Service. That's success. Furnished with money and a little fame, even the elderly, if they care to, may partake of friendly diversions. That's pleasure. It might happen once in a while that something I said or wrote was sufficiently heeded for me to persuade myself that it represented a serious impact on our time. That's fulfillment. Yet, I say to you, and I beg you to believe me, multiply these tiny triumphs by millions, add them all up together, and they are nothing, less than nothing. Indeed, a positive impediment measured against one drop of that living water Christ offers to the spiritually thirsty, irrespective of who or what they are.[21]

Discussing the meaning of the cross in the context of pain and suffering, Zacharias quotes James Stewart's

21. Malcolm Muggeridge, *Jesus Rediscovered.* Garden City, NY: Doubleday, 1969, p.77. Used by permission.

expository on the apostle Paul's quote from Psalm 68:18, "He led captivity captive.":

> It is a glorious phrase—"He led captivity captive." The very triumphs of His foes, it means, He used for their defeat. He compelled their dark achievements to subserve His ends, not theirs. They nailed Him to the tree, not knowing that by that very act they were bringing the world to His feet. They gave Him a cross, not guessing that He would make it a throne. They flung Him outside the gates to die, not knowing that in that very moment they were lifting up all the gates of the universe, to let the King come in. They thought to root out His doctrines, not understanding that they were implanting imperishably in the hearts of men the very name they intended to destroy. They thought that they had God with His back to the wall, pinned and helpless and defeated: they did not know that it was God Himself who had tracked them down. He did not conquer in spite of the dark mystery of evil. He conquered through it.[22]

September 15, 1999 —Singapore

We berthed at Singapore last night at about 1000 hours. Just to our East now is Borneo and to our West is Sumatra. Malaysia is split in two, sharing part of the East island with Borneo and the tiny oil-rich kingdom of Brunei. As hoped, I took shore leave and visited the Raffles Hotel and nearby Raffles Centre and Raffles Place. The changes to the neighborhood were so overwhelming that nothing was familiar. The Hotel itself was not as I had remembered it, with many changes. That old British colonial charm remained, however, like the antiquity that it is. I was with one of the Kiribati crewmen, Bwaauto Tebikau, and not having the time for

22. James Stewart, *The Strong Name*. Grand Rapids: Baker, 1972. p.55. Used by permission.

leisurely dining, we chose to have lunch in the food court of the ultra-modern Westin Centre across the street.

We are scheduled to leave Singapore this evening sometime, as soon as the loading process is complete. The Cho Yang Atlas will be fully loaded with Asian consumer goods going to principal markets in Western Europe. Because of the imbalance in trade, the ship will turn around and bring back to Asia at least some empty containers. Containers now block the view from my front cabin windows for the first time on this voyage, but I still have two windows open on the starboard side.This will be the "long haul" for the Cho Yang Atlas, from Asia to Europe nonstop. Next stop will be LeHavre, with only a pause as we queue with a convoy of other ships to pass through the Suez Canal. As we leave Singapore we will head northwest through the Strait of Malacca to the Andaman Sea, thence East into the Indian Ocean. Our route takes us just to the South of Columbo and then into the Arabian Sea.

The terminal here in Singapore is a vast beehive of activity. The containers are stacked six to ten high in an area that would cover several square miles. Singapore and Hong Kong are the most important and busiest ports for exports from Asia. On the shuttle buses to the entrance gates of this giant complex were seaman on shore leave from all over Asia, but most of them from the Philippines. Returning to the ship with me on the shuttle were three Filipino and four Kiribati crewmen. This day gave me a new insight into the lives of these seamen. They bought gifts for their families, stereo equipment and compact discs to enjoy in their cabins, and phone cards to make calls home. Joseph Conrad, in *The Heart of Darkness*, describes the men who "follow the sea":

> Their minds are of the stay-at-home order, and their home is always with them—the ship; and so is their country—the sea. One ship is very much like another, and the sea is always the same. In the immutability of their surroundings the foreign shores, the foreign faces, the changing immensity of life, glide past, veiled not by a sense of mystery but by a slightly disdainful ignorance; for there is nothing mysterious to a seaman unless it be the sea itself, which is the mistress of his existence and as inscrutable as Destiny.

Some of the ships on which they came to Singapore were the APL Philippines, CCNI Arica, Tiger Creek, Jaru Bhum, Nant Bhum—Bangkok, Phong Chau-Haiphong, Alam Java—II, and the Kota Melati, the ship names themselves indicative of the diverse world from which they come.

September 16, 1999

I am watching a magnificent golden disk rise this morning on the southeastern horizon as our ship methodically makes its way up the Strait of Malacca. We are only a few degrees off coast from the city I always thought has the most poetic and exotic name in Asia—Kuala Lampur, Malaysia. We have calm seas but an approaching storm. I am watching flashes of light in the distant thunderheads; the sea and distant horizon set a dramatic stage for observing storms and the creative glory of God.

Last night I awoke sometime shortly after we had departed Singapore. Watching the lights of ships on the starboard side, I noticed a string of lights traveling in our same direction but faster. Suddenly I realized it was a train—and, yes, of course it was the Bangkok-Rangoon-Singapore

---

23. Joseph Conrad, *The Heart of Darkness*. London: J. M. Dent (Everyman), 1899 (reprint, 1998). Copyright expired.

extension of the Orient Express, which is still in service. I had read about it on the Internet shortly before leaving home for this voyage. Also, the flashing light of an airplane high in the night sky drew my attention to the stars. I turned out all lights in the cabin and spent long moments pondering the heavens. There in the southeastern sky I located Andromeda, Pegasus, and Cassiopeia.

Viewing the stars, I thought of what Whittaker Chambers had written in the final chapter of his book *Witness*—that he took his son out to look at the stars at night in hopes he would never lose his sense of reverence and wonder. Whittaker wrote:

> Now and again, I remind him that what we can just make out as a faint haze is another universe—the radiance of fifty thousand suns whose light had left its source thirty-four thousand years before it brushes the miracle of our straining sight. . . . I want him to see for himself upon the scale of the universes that God, the soul, faith, are not simple matters, and that no easy or ingenuous view of them is possible. I want him to remember that God Who is a God of Love is also the God of a world that includes the atom bomb and virus, the minds that contrived and use or those who suffer them; and that the problem of good and evil is not more simple than the immensity of the worlds. . . . I want him to know, in that dark, continuous struggle, that it is by his soul, and his soul alone, that he may sometimes glimpse, if only roughly, the hour of the night and his direction in it. I want him to understand, when he lifts up his eyes, that against the range of space and cold his soul, and his soul alone, is life for which, in the morning and the evening, he gives thanks to God to Whom it ties him. I want him to know that it is his soul, and his soul alone,

> that makes it possible for him to bear, without dying of his own mortality, the faint light of Hercules' fifty thousand suns."

That's why I appreciate biblical accounts of prophets, shepherds and wise men watching the stars with awe and adoration. The Scriptures reveal that they searched the heavens for signs and reminders that God exists, that He remained unchanged, and that He still had control of the mysteries of their universe. The Psalms express their yearning for a personal relationship with Him. "My soul yearns, even faints for the courts of the Lord; my heart and my flesh cry out for the living God" wrote the Psalmist (84:2). I ponder those lines and make them my own and send up petitions to heaven that some of the shepherds' wisdom accrues to me also, so that I too shall not lose my sense of wonder with all Creation.

At one time this morning I counted eleven large tankers on either side of the Cho Yang Atlas, carrying petrol from the Middle East to fuel the industry of Asia. It is nearly noon now and not once all morning have we been without the company of tankers along this narrow strait that is a principal sea lane from Europe to Asia. We are destined to see even more in the Red Sea. One of the largest of the tankers, one of Egyptian Lines, bore the simple name Nile.

It is now the end of the day and I have returned from a walk that took me six times around the ship. That's well over a mile. We are still passing freighters, both tankers and containers, going in both directions. Captain Mahnke told me that tomorrow morning we will be headed due East in the Indian Ocean. Also, once again we set our clocks back an hour tonight, so there's an extra hour's sleep in the morning for those who want more pillow time. As dusk falls, I'll bid my computer adieu and read myself to sleep listening to Bizet's "L'Arlesienne Suites 1 and 2" played by the Slovak Philharmonic.

September 17, 1999

Overcast skies this morning but a calm Indian Ocean now as we head due East toward Columbo. I consult my atlas each morning to fix in my mind exactly where I am on the planet. Rangoon, Burma, now Myanmar, is due North ten degrees, and the Bay of Bengal and Bangladesh are another five degrees further North. Both Bangladesh and Calcutta are about 1,500 miles North of the Cho Yang Atlas this morning. Today we will pass just South of the Nicobar Islands, staying at latitude six degrees North all the way until we have passed the Indian subcontinent. We are on schedule to arrive at Suez next Thursday morning, seven days hence.

I toured Burma in 1970, making a trek to the fabled pagodas of Pagan and Mandalay. The visit was memorable but not the most pleasant. The airplane on which our tour group flew there crashed at the next stop after we deplaned. The gondola we boarded on the Irawaddy River sprung a fatal leak and sunk, leaving us to wade to safety in mud to our knees.

Rudyard Kipling rhapsodized about the "road to Mandalay where the flying fishes play." He must have been at sea when he wrote that poem because biographers say he never set foot in Burma. I was also once in Calcutta briefly en route to Nepal, but I saw all the misery I could manage without leaving the airport. This was the place where Mother Theresa picked up the sick and dying from the dustbins. May she rest in peace! I never see or hear the name Bangladesh without being reminded of the cyclones that almost annually devastate the country that one economist labeled a fourth-world place.

It is now late afternoon on our first day on the Indian Ocean. It has remained overcast all day and the ocean swells have been heaviest so far on this voyage, but still somewhat subdued. The ship has rocked from side to side a little all day but gently, and I've had no motion sickness. Since we are directly in the sea-lane from Europe to Southeast Asia, we've been in sight of ships all day long. Captain Mahnke told me at lunch that we had passed our sister ship, the Cho Yang Ace. I said, "Ah, but we're number one, jah?" And he chuckled. Also word came that while we were in Singapore a typhoon hit Hong Kong and claimed at least one ship.

September 18, 1999

> The seas have lifted up, O Lord,
> the seas have lifted up their voice,
> the seas have lifted up their pounding waves.
> Mightier than the thunder of the great waters,
> Mightier than the breakers of the sea,
> The Lord on high is mighty. (Ps. 93:3–4)

We have clear skies this morning as we near Sri Lanka. Out of "nowhere" a small container ship, the Novia, has seemingly pulled up beside us, but no, we are just passing it ever so slowly, for we had pulled up close to it. The ships normally are too far away to read their names, but occasionally we have a close encounter.

I finished reading Jules Verne's *Around the World in Eighty Days* last night. I read it years ago but had forgotten the ending. Would Phileas Fogg win his bet and be back in London at the Reform Club on Saturday, the 21st of

December at a quarter before nine in the evening? Here's the exciting finale:

> One minute more and the wager would be won! Andrew Stuart and his partners suspended their game. They left their cards, and counted the seconds.
>
> At the fortieth second, nothing. At the fiftieth second, still nothing.
>
> At the fifty-fifth, a loud cry was heard in the street, followed by applause, hurrahs, and some fierce growls.
>
> The players rose from their seats.
>
> At the fifty-seventh second the door of the saloon opened; and the pendulum had not beat the sixtieth second when Phileas Fogg appeared, followed by an excited crowd who had forced their way through the club doors, and in his calm voice, said, "Here I am, gentlemen!"
>
> Yes: Phileas Fogg in person."
>
> Phileas Fogg had won his wager and had made his trip around the world in eighty days. . . . The eccentric gentleman had throughout displayed all his marvelous qualities of coolness and exactitude. But what then? What had he really gained by all this trouble? What had he brought back from this long and weary journey? Nothing, say you? . . . Truly, would you not for less than that make the tour around the world?

We have six-foot swells this morning. I've been out on the main deck observing the flying fish and the whitecaps. From the ship's deck, you can see the ocean waves repeat themselves *ad infinitum* in a definite pattern—sparkling canyons of water as far as the eye can see. They are mesmerizing with their dazzling caps of briny foam. Occasionally you can see jellyfish and other sea life near the surface and floating by a surprising lot of buoyant trash. The ship's passing causes only a trickle in the grand scheme of things.

Moments ago we passed alongside the tanker Provence, headed also toward Europe. Will we meet again in LeHavre? I suspect so.

It is noon and we are skirting Sri Lanka, plainly visible as the coastline fronts the starboard side. In my fourth grade geography class I learned about this place, then called Ceylon, famous for its tea. My Peace Corps friends described it as a true garden of Eden, abloom year round with tropical flowers. Nevertheless, this former Dutch colony is another troubled third-world place better seen these days from a distant freighter.

We will now begin a northward route into the Arabian Sea and should reach the Gulf of Aden in a couple of days. The next land we see will be Yemen, not Somalia. Captain Mahnke informed me that the ship keeps well away from the Somali coast because of piracy.

This afternoon we passed the tanker India and the Deepwater 2–Kingston, perhaps an ocean research ship, both close enough that I could read their names with my binoculars. Also, I saw unmistakable whale spouts this afternoon. Now the question is: what kind of whale? From a description of the spouts of the blue, finback, humpback, right, and sperm whales, I believe the spouts I saw yesterday must have been those of the right whale.

September 19, 1999

> How many are your works, O Lord. In wisdom You made them. All the earth is full of Your creatures. There is the sea, vast and spacious, teaming with creatures beyond number, living things both large and small. There the ships go to and fro, and the leviathan, which You formed to frolic there. (Ps. 104:24–26)

Clear skies and a calm sea this morning as we pass just North of the Maldive Islands. The first vessel I saw was a tiny fishing boat, so small I needed binoculars to discover it. Near Taiwan the fishermen seemed to congregate in sight of one another. Here, they fish solo. Yesterday I wondered what would happen if they happened to miscalculate their fuel needs or had engine failure and could not get back to land. And how do they escape the impromptu storms? Captain Mahnke told me that some of these fishing vessels remain at sea overnight and negotiating among them can be hazardous. These tiny fishing boats look so vulnerable so far out to sea with no land in sight. And how do they find their way to shore on a limitless horizon? Intuition must be their principal means of navigation or perhaps these, too, have a simplified form of GPS.[24]

Last night I read again the story of Jonah. I am trying to place the biblical stories within their geographical contexts as I prepare to pass that way next week through the Red Sea and Mediterranean. At the same time, I want to refresh my memory about the biblical events. In Egypt, on the starboard side of the Gulf of Suez, there will be Mt. Sinai ,where Moses received the Ten Commandments (Ex. 19–20); in modern Turkey, Mt Ararat, where Noah's Ark came to rest (Gen. 8:4), though our ship will be far South of this point in Turkey; Joppa (now Jaffa), where Jonah under protest set out for Ninevah (Jon. 1:3); Malta, where the apostle Paul was shipwrecked (Acts 28:1); and Rome itself, where tradition says that both Peter and Paul were martyred.

Of course, there are Jordon, Palestine, and Israel, where all events of the New Testament and most in the Old Testament transpired. Tourists to modern Turkey can visit the ruins of the seven cities addressed in Revelation; as a U.S.

24. GPS—Global Positioning System (navigation by satellites).

Air Force officer, I visited Ephesus, Smyrna, Laodicea, Thyatira, and Thessalonika in 1971.

In Herman Melville's *Moby Dick*, Father Mapple's sermon about Jonah's grand adventure is delightful reading, more dramatic than the biblical account itself.

> . . . God came upon him in the whale and swallowed him down to living gulfs of doom, and with swift slantings tore him along "into the midst of the seas," where the eddying depths sucked him ten thousand fathoms down, and "the weeds were wrapped about his head," and all the watery world of woe bowled over him. . . . [E]ven then, God heard the engulphed, repenting prophet when he cried. Then God spake to the fish; and from the shuddering cold and blackness of the sea, the whale came breeching up towards the warm and pleasant sun, and all the delights of air and earth; and "vomited out Jonah upon the dry land."[25]

Athens is the city where Paul, greatly distressed to see that the city was full of idols, noticed an altar inscribed to "an unknown God." He told a group of Epicurean and Stoic philosophers about the Lord God Jehovah and of the resurrected Christ (Acts 17:16–31). F.W. Boreham put Paul's speech in proper perspective when he wrote:

> The climax of Philosophy was reached on Mars' Hill. Paul stood in Athens, amid the schools of the philosophers. He told them the story of Jesus, Wrote on their hearts every word, Told them the story so precious, Sweetest that ever was heard; Told how the angels in chorus Sang as they welcomed his birth Glory to God in highest Peace and good tidings on earth! That was the

25. Herman Melville, *Moby Dick*. London: Penguin Books, 1851, Reprint, 1994. p. 62. Copyright expired.

> climax of Philosophy; its long, long quest had ended at the feet of Jesus![26]

Other places along the shores of the Mediterranean were the scenes of significant moments in the life of Israel and the early church: Corinth, Philippi, Damascus, the two Antiochs, Cyprus, and others.

Tiny Albania on the Adriatic is the birthplace of a modern saint, Mother Theresa. This, along with its neighbor, Montenegro, is also the place to which thousands of Kosovars early this year fled from ethnic cleansing. This was only the most recent of the long centuries of wars staged in the Mediterranean. The Mediterranean, of course, was the "cradle of civilization." The Assyrian, Persian, Grecian, and Roman empires all found the Mediterranean world a stage set for pomp and glory; all of them would grow dim and expire, but not without making major contributions to western civilization in religion, music, architecture, science, philosophy, law, government, and literature, the greater part of which came about under the influence of Christianity.

September 20, 1999

> For as high as the heavens are above the earth, so great is His love for those who fear Him; as far as the east is from the west, so far has he removed our transgressions from us. (Ps. 103:11–12)

Spend days and weeks at sea traveling from West to East and you get some idea of what the Psalmist means. East and West are too far apart to ever meet. This morning we keep a steady pace of about 23.7 knots toward the

26. Excerpted from F.W. Boreham's *Ships of Pearl.* (New York: The Abingdon Press, 1935, p. 288). Copyright expired.

Gulf of Aden, Somalia, Yemen and Djibouti, arrival time at the Red Sea in a couple of days. Our traveling speed translates to about 650 miles per day. To travel all the way around the globe is roughly 25,000 miles, if you could travel unobstructed in a straight line. I look at the world map outside the officers' mess and see that we have come a long, long way. The sky this morning is a mixed palette of thunderhead soapsuds, patches of blue, and strings of serous clouds; the sea is relatively calm with only scattered patches of foam.

Every day at sea is a unique experience. Today walking on the main deck, and later on the forecastle, was like walking on an active earthquake with each step a cautious balancing ballet step to keep oneself upright. Suddenly the swells grew larger and from the forecastle I had the sensation of the ship climbing a hill. You look out on a concave sphere of water and realize this is the "big blue" in the "big blue marble" the astronauts described; somewhere out there you could drop off the end of the earth.

I keep seeing flying fish and watching for spouting whales, or anything else of interest on the horizon. But the sea itself and the water-colored canopy of sky with their changing patterns and tints like faded quilts provide endless interest and fascination.

For most sailors, no doubt some of the enchantment of the ocean seeps through, but I see them busy about their chores, with little time to stop and ponder their spectacular environment. I suspect that for most, a seaman's day is routine, with the sea evoking a sameness that often borders on boredom. For other sailors, however, the sea is an artist's workshop of poetry and music and great pastel seascapes and long-ago and far-away thoughts of departures and homecomings and so much else that only the imagination could guess.

September 21, 1999—Gulf of Aden

Be at rest once more, O my soul, for the Lord has been good to you. (Ps. 116:7)

The big events for today will be our arrival in the Gulf of Aden at about 1700. At the same time we will have a barbeque supper on the forecastle. That means a lot of work for the cook, steward, and many of the crew, who must carry tables, chairs, dishes, etc. the equivalent of about two city blocks, then back again. I have offered to help but my offer was not accepted. Earlier in the voyage Captain Mahnke informed me that from the forecastle in the Gulf of Aden we may be able to see the phosphorescent lights of the sea life when darkness sets in.

It is quite windy, with giant whitecaps on the Arabian Sea this morning—our highest swells yet on this voyage. Not a cloud in the sky, but there's a fine overhead gauzy mist filtering the sun. Also, on deck this morning I noticed it is perhaps ten degrees cooler. We are headed northward in latitude now, after all, and it is just two days away from the official beginning of autumn. Electrician Rey Cajita (Mindanao, Philippines) is installing a heater in my cabin and I know the added warmth will be welcome when we get to the Mediterranean.

2030 Hours in the Gulf of Aden. Captain Mahnke and I have just returned to our cabins after the barbecue on the forecastle. He informed me of a major earthquake in Taiwan, where we were just a week ago. The fiesta was a welcome diversion. Menu included barbecued beef, pork, chicken, and fish, fried rice, potato salad, a huge fruit bowl of apples, bananas, tangerines, oranges, prunes, walnuts, and more, with beer and coke for beverages. Third Mate

Joel Semino had decorated the fiesta area with national flags and other signal flags. These parties are a major morale booster for the crew. This passenger enjoyed the party immensely.

The clocks go back another hour tonight; then there will be one more time adjustment when we get into the Mediterranean. I now shut down my computer with the slumbering sounds of Allegri's "Miserere mei, Deus."

Tomorrow—the Red Sea!

September 22, 1999

> My eyes stay open through the watches of the night, that I may meditate upon your promises. (Ps. 119:148)

> In the night I remember your name, O Lord, and I will keep Your law. (Ps. 119:55)

These verses of Scripture, although no doubt written by shepherds keeping watch over flocks of sheep at night, reminded me of the seamen responsible for safe passage of the ship. The safety of all on the ship requires that their eyes stay open. Watches for the ship are primarily the responsibility of the Chief Mate, 2nd Mate, and 3rd Mate. The watches are in increments of four hours beginning at 0000 hours (midnight) and continuing through the day. In passing through time changes of longitude, the officer on night watch will sometimes have five hours of duty when clocks are being set back, and only three hours of duty when clocks are being set forward. The prescribed time to change the clock is 0100 hours.

I will be watching today for landfall. We should see Yemen on the starboard side of the ship, Somalia and Djibouti to port. As soon as we pass into the Red Sea, Ethiopia and Eritrea will be on the port side. Sometime tomorrow, Sudan will be on the port side, with Saudi Arabia on the starboard side. Egypt straddles the Suez and immigrations officials will board the ship at the entrance to the Canal.

Preparing to pass through Egypt, I have been reading the biblical accounts of Moses and the wanderings of the children of Israel after the Exodus. The writer of Deuteronomy asks questions that are contemporary:

> Ask now about the former days, long before your time, from the day God created man on the earth; ask from one end of the heavens to the other. Has anything so great as this ever happened, or has anything like this ever been heard of? Has any other people heard the voice of God speaking out of fire, as you have, and lived? Has any god ever tried to take for himself one nation out of another nation, by testings, by miraculous signs and wonders, by war, by a mighty hand and an outstretched arm, or by great and awesome deeds, like all the things the Lord your God did for you in Egypt before your very eyes? You were shown these things so that you might know that the Lord is God; besides Him there is no other. From heaven He made you hear His voice to discipline you. On earth He showed you His great fire, and you heard His words from out of the fire. . . . Acknowledge and take to heart this day that the Lord is God in heaven above and on earth below. There is no other. (Deut. 4:32–39)

We arrived at the entrance to the Red Sea about 1415 this afternoon. The ship took an immediate turn northwestward, so now we will be moving to cooler days. The coastline of Yemen is misty, but the city of Al Mukha, Yemen with its white buildings and minarets gleamed in the afternoon sunshine. On the forecastle this afternoon I watched a school of porpoises frolicking in the water. I had a moment of real serendipity late today when a huge migration of white gulls passed the ship, flying South. It reminded me of a similar moment years ago when I saw the sky pink with flamingos over the soda lakes of the Great Rift Valley in Kenya.

How came the name "Red" Sea? I wondered and consulted Rachel Carson:

> Seasonal abundance of certain forms (of algae and other microorganisms) containing reddish or brown pigments may cause the "red water" known from ancient times in many parts of the world, and so common is this condition in some enclosed seas that they owe their name to it—the Red Sea and the Vermilion Sea are examples.[27]

What I see out the portholes of my cabin with my flawed color vision is a very calm sea tinged with maroon. I'm also reminded that it has been called the Red Sea since biblical times.

At dinner tonight Captain Mahnke said Taiwan had a second earthquake that has caused major port disruption, with more than a hundred ships in queue. I count my blessings that our timing in Taiwan was better. I shut down my laptop today with the music of Quarantotto/Sartori: "Time to Say Goodbye." Was that not one of the themes for the film Out of Africa?

September 23, 1999

> The Lord does whatever pleases Him
> In heaven and in earth, in the seas and in their depths.
> He makes the clouds rise from the ends of the earth.
> He sends lightning with the rain and brings out the wind
> From His storehouses. (Ps. 135:6–7)

27. Rachel Carson, *Ibid*, p. 34.

The Psalmist who wrote those lyrics could not have known that modern science and meteorology would prove accurate his words "[God] brings out the wind from His storehouses." The storehouses of the wind have been proven to have their genesis in tropical seas, where solar energy warms the water that meets with the colder ocean currents. The Prime Mover, of course, predetermines it all.

From scientific journals I learned that ocean waters are constantly on the move. Great ocean currents contribute to the heat transport from the tropics to the poles, partially equalizing Earth surface temperatures. Ocean circulation patterns influence climate and living conditions for plants and animals, even on land. These patterns also affect the routes taken by ships as they carry goods and people between continents. Ocean currents flow in complex patterns affected by wind, the water's salinity and heat content, bottom topography, and the earth's rotation. These ocean currents and the resulting global circulation patterns are of enormous interest to scientists studying Earth systems and global change issues.

This morning I watched a shadowy orange disk rise on the horizon through dense mist that still obscures the land—Saudi Arabia now. We are now very near Jiddah and Mecca. On our port side, Sudan. The surface of the sea is a smooth ripple and the ship almost seems stationary though we progress at a steady pace.

I have just returned from my morning exercise on the forecastle—a nice hike just to get there and back. The ship's anchors are stowed there. Anchors, of course, have provided an ageless and noteworthy metaphor for writers and philosophers. Joseph Conrad paints an accurate description in his *The Mirror of the Sea*:

> From first to last the seaman's thoughts are very much concerned with his anchors. It is not so much that the anchor is a symbol of hope as that it is the heaviest object that he has to handle on board his ship at sea in the usual routine of duties. The beginning and the end of every passage are marked distinctly by work about the ship's anchors. . . . [T]hose emblems of hope make company for the look-out man in the night watches; and so the days glide by, with a long rest for those characteristically shaped pieces of iron, reposing forward, . . . waiting for their work on the other side of the world somewhere, while the ship carries them on with a great rush and splutter of foam underneath, and the sprays of the open sea rust their heavy limbs.[28]

I was thinking today of how different this voyage might have been for me had there been other passengers. I was prepared to re-learn how to play bridge, to swap travel stories, to pick the brains of fellow passengers. As it is, I have had to be totally self-reliant in keeping my mind occupied while having no real shipboard responsibilities other than to get myself to the officers' mess on time. I've had some superb reading material and my world has been stretched immeasurably, with time to ponder the imponderables. Also, I've been able to spend some quality time on this manuscript.

September 24, 1999

> Give thanks to the Lord, for He is good. His love endures forever . . . who by His understanding made the heavens . . . who spread out the earth upon the waters . . . who made the great lights . . . the sun to govern the day . . . the

28. Joseph Conrad, *The Mirror of the Sea*. Oxford: Oxford University Press, 1988, pp. 15–16. Copyright expired.

> moon and stars to govern the night . . . to Him who divided the Red Sea asunder and brought Israel through the midst of it . . . but swept Pharaoh and his army into the Red Sea. (Ps. 136:1–15)

We are very near the Suez this morning as the sun rises majestically over Egypt to the East beneath a buttermilk sky. Out my cabin windows are four tankers passing in review. We expect to be boarded by as many as five customs/immigrations officials from Egypt. They will stay on board overnight and go with us through the canal tomorrow. The transit takes about ten hours. Unlike the Panama Canal with locks, the Suez is simply a narrow passageway through Egypt with a lake in the center. Northbound and southbound traffic pass in the lake where the channel is wide enough to accommodate both. The number of ships is regulated from both ends and passage is coordinated. We will anchor overnight and begin the transit at 0800 tomorrow.

Sometime this afternoon I am hoping to get a glimpse of Mt. Sinai. Whether or not the antitheist mind wants to believe that God spoke to Moses from a burning bush or prescribed to him the Ten Commandments, the moral code of the civilized world has been handed down to us from those events recorded in Exodus and Deuteronomy. Biblical archaeologists have been finding substantive proof that all the events recorded in the Old Testament are factual. Those scruples recorded in the Old Testament were the foundation for civil law in all of the western world beginning in the first century. However glamorously Hollywood may portray deviations from the Ten Commandments, it still makes a difference in the world whether one lies, cheats, steals, covets, murders, or worships anything made by mankind. Deviations make our world a place less livable.

I so very well remember the first six years of elementary school where on the walls in front of me were posted in large print the Ten Commandments: "I am the Lord thy God. . . . Thou shalt have no other gods before me. . . ." They made an indelible impression on this six-year-old boy. And I think it is tragic that our American young people today do not have the same moral code blazed into their minds as they begin the journey of life.

Even if I do not catch a glimpse of Mt. Sinai, I will be grateful for the reminders of what happened in this Egyptian desert, of the way God provided for His people Israel, of the way He has always kept His magnificent promises to Abraham and his descendants. And I will always be grateful that He provided a way for me, too, to partake of His promises and unfathomable love. Laudate Jesu Christus!

I made my morning trek to the forecastle and discovered that we have high winds and heavy swells this morning. It reminds me that God is capable of dividing the sea whenever He chooses.

September 25, 1999

> He determines the number of the stars and calls them each by name. Great is our Lord and mighty in power; His understanding has no limit. (Ps. 147:4–5)

The sky is overcast this morning with clouds and polluted air. The sun is making a valiant effort to show its face, but blushes and hides behind the clouds, then peeps out every so often. Last night a full platinum moon ascended over the horizon behind a curtain of smoke above the oil rigs, then rose to clear skies and lit up the Sinai desert.

We began our transit of the Suez this morning at 0600, two hours sooner than scheduled. Surprisingly, the canal is no wider than a large muddy creek, except that midway is a lake where ships may pass. There are oil derricks on the starboard side of the ship as far as the eye can see on the South end of the canal. On the port side are drab buildings that appear to be military garrisons or public works buildings of some sort. There are palm trees here. On the southern end of the canal, the landscape is bleak with sandy soil and little vegetation or crops. On the northern end are flooded rice paddies.

All along the canal are the military bunkers used by the Israelis when they occupied the entire Sinai Peninsula. I recall the long history of conflict in this area, going all the way back to Moses and the Pharaohs. Even now, along the port side, I see bunkers, lookout posts, and men in uniform standing guard. For what? A centuries-old fear of retaliation born out of vengeance keeps the nerves on edge. The Suez Canal itself is steeped with history, and my interest is whetted to research and know more about it. Among other things I know that ships were sunk in the canal during the Israeli-Arab war in 1967. The canal was impassable for eight years. Captain Mahnke told me of two German ships that were in the deep-water anchorage at the time and remained there in exile for eight years. When the canal was opened, they returned to Hamburg as heroes, the Elbe River lined with thousands of people to cheer their return.

On the port side I saw the ruins of what had been pontoon bridges used to facilitate military warfare on either side of the canal. Also, Egypt had a brand new asphalt road running the full length of the canal. I kept thinking that I had helped pay for the road with my taxes. I have never been able to comprehend the rationale behind enormous outlays of American foreign aid to these countries in the Middle East. Paul Theroux, discussing the political problems of Syria, Jordan, Lebanon, Palestine, and Israel put the matter in perspective:

> These countries were so small! One of the more marvelous atrocities of our time was the way in which the self-created problems of these countries, and their arrogant way of dealing with them, made them seem larger, like an angry child standing on its tiptoes. They were expensive to operate, too, they had vast armies; they indulged in loud and ridiculously long-winded denunciations of their neighbors. All this contributed to the illusion that they were massive. But, no, they were tiny, irritating, shameless and vindictive; and they occupied the world's attention way out of proportion to their size or their importance. They had been magnified by lobbyists and busybody groups.[29]

The Suez Canal and its strategic importance for world trade is, of course, the principal basis for foreign aid, along with the area's massive reserves of petroleum. The Suez acts as a kind of catalyst for so much of what happens politically throughout the Middle East and Asia. And the U.S. is a beneficiary in the equation, along with all the other western democracies.

The Suez transit took eleven hours and we are now in the Mediterranean, headed for LeHavre, with a scheduled arrival time of 0600 October 1—just five days.

"The Mediterranean is beautiful in a different way from the ocean," wrote Victor Hugo, "but it is as beautiful. The ocean has its clouds, its fogs, its glaucous glassy billows, its sand dunes in Flanders, its immense vaults, its magnificent

---

29. Paul Theroux, *The Pillars of Hercules*. London: Penguin Books, 1996. p. 456. Used by permission.

tides. The Mediterranean lies wholly in the sun; you feel it by the inexpressible unity that lies at the foundation of its beauty. It has a tawny stern coast, the hills and the rocks of which seem rounded or sculptured by Phidias, so harmoniously is the shore wedded to gracefulness."

The word Mediterranean means "middle of the earth." Early civilizations thought of it as the very center of the earth in the days when it was believed that the earth was flat. Beyond the Pillars of Hercules was a river that circled the earth, but a region too frightening to explore.

The Mediterranean world is such a repository of great art and architecture of the world that to speak of any is to discount the importance of others. One towering work, however, Antonio Gaudi's masterpiece in Barcelona, the Sagrada Familia, deserves comment. Colm Toibin, in his book on Barcelona, tells the story of Gaudi having been interrogated by a visiting bishop. Why had Gaudi decorated the tops of towers that no one would ever see? Gaudi replied, "Your Grace, the angels will see them."

Our route will take us near Malta where the apostle Paul was shipwrecked. Here in the Mediterranean, of course, was where all of Paul's missionary journeys took place. He visited such places as Corinth, Athens, Ephesus, Antioch, Smyrna, and Macedonia, taking the gospel to the Gentiles. Later he wrote the letters to the struggling churches in those places. We sense the power of his letters when we read his words: "For the foolishness of God is wiser than man's wisdom, and the weakness of God is stronger than man's strength." (1 Cor. 1:25)

Joseph Conrad dramatized a voyage on the Mediterranean with this romantic description in his *The Mirror of the Sea*:

Happy he who, like Ulysses, has made an adventurous voyage, and there is no such seas for adventurous voyages as the Mediterranean—the inland sea which the ancients looked upon as so vast and so full of wonders. And, indeed, it was terrible and wonderful; for it is we alone who, swayed by the audacity of our minds and the tremors of our hearts, are the sole artisans of all the wonder and romance of the world.

It was for the Mediterranean sailors that fair-haired sirens sang among the black rocks seething in white foam and mysterious voices spoke in the darkness above the moving wave—voices menacing, seductive, or prophetic, like that voice heard at the beginning of the Christian era by the master of an African vessel in the Gulf of Serta, whose calm nights are full of strange murmurs and flitting shadows. It called him by name, bidding him go and tell all men that the great god Pan was dead. But the great legend of the Mediterranean, the legend of traditional song and grave history lives, fascinating and immortal, in our minds.

The dark and fearful sea of the subtle Ulysses' wanderings, agitated by the wrath of Olympian gods, harbouring on its isles the fury of strange monsters and the wiles of strange women; the highway of heroes and sages, of warriors, pirates, and saints; the workaday sea of Carthaginian merchants and the pleasure lake of the Roman Caesars, claims the veneration of every seaman as the historical home of that spirit of open defiance against the great waters of the earth which is the very soul of his calling. . . . The steep shores of the Mediterranean favoured the beginners of humanity's most daring enterprises, and the enchanting inland sea of classic adventure has led mankind gently from headland to headland, from bay to bay, from island to island, out into the promise of world-wide oceans beyond the Pillars of Hercules.[30]

September 26, 1999

In the crown of Italy's boot is the small hill village of Aliano, a place I very much hope to visit someday. Because of his anti-fascist views, Carlo Levi, a Florentine Jew and a medical doctor, was banished to Aliano in 1935 for an entire year, where he languished under house arrest. There he served as the village doctor, painted pictures, and got to know everyone in the village. He kept a journal, and after he left he wrote the classic memoir *Christ Stopped at Eboli*. Librarians find it unclassifiable because it is a combination of travel, philosophy, anthropology, and autobiography. Levi took the title of the book from a local maxim in Aliano (called Gagliano in his book). The villagers thought of themselves as heathens living on a crumbling hill. They thought that Christ had not come so far as their village but had stopped at Eboli, fifty miles away.

I identify with Levi and his book somewhat at this time because I feel a bit as though I have been in exile for the extent of this voyage, albeit an exile of my own choosing. Such is life for all sailors. They have chosen a vocation requiring exile from their families, friends and associates, from all that is a normal part of being on land. Perhaps it is in our exiles that we focus on what is worthwhile and make our best value judgments about life, realign priorities, and like Tennyson's Ulysses, challenge ourselves for something new and worthwhile. It was my high school English teachers Mrs. B. B. Bailey and Mrs. Hazel Vaughan who, with their enthusiasm for the arts, instilled in me this appreciation for great poetry, full of imagery and lessons

30. Joseph Conrad, *The Mirror of the Sea.* Oxford: Oxford University Press, pp. 151–152. Copyright expired.

for living. I owe them much. Mrs. Bailey introduced me to Tennyson's famous poem *Ulysses*[31] and it has ever since been one of my favorites. The poem is a metaphor of life's challenges for those growing older; it borrows from Homer's Odyssey the theme of a Mediterranean voyage.

Alfred Lord Tennyson (1809–1892)
Ulysses

It little profits that an idle king,
By this still hearth, among these barren crags,
Match'd with an aged wife, I mete and dole
Unequal laws unto a savage race,
That hoard, and sleep, and feed, and know not me.
I cannot rest from travel: I will drink
Life to the lees: All times I have enjoy'd
Greatly, have suffer'd greatly, both with those
That loved me, and alone, on shore, and when

31. The poem was written soon after the death of one of his friends, Arthur Hallam. Tennyson wrote that Hallam's death gave him the feeling about the need of going forward and braving the struggle of life "perhaps more simply than anything in (his other well-known poem) *In Memoriam*". It was Hallam who had encouraged Tennyson to a study of Dante and *Ulysses* was based on a passage in Dante's *Inferno*, canto XXVI. Both poets recalled Homer's *Odyssey,* XI, 100–37, where the ghost foretold Ulysses' fortune. Tennyson praises Ulysses' restless aspiration, whereas Dante condemned his curiosity and presumption. Rainy Hyades is a reference to a group of stars that rise with the sun in spring at the rainy season. Ithaca was the island where Ulysses was king. The "western baths" was the poetic place where stars seemed to plunge into the ocean. The phrase "wash us down" referred to Homer's imagining the sea outside the Pillars of Hercules (Gibraltar) as a river encompassing the earth, and on the West plunging down a vast chasm where was the entrance of Hades. The Happy Isles were the islands of the blessed, imagined to lie to the West of the Pillars of Hercules, i.e., in the Atlantic.

Thro' scudding drifts the rainy Hyades
Vext the dim sea: I am become a name;
For always roaming with a hungry heart
Much have I seen and known; cities of men
And manners, climates, councils, governments,
Myself not least, but honour'd of them all;
And drunk delight of battle with my peers,
Far on the ringing plains of windy Troy.
I am a part of all that I have met;
Yet all experience is an arch wherethro'
Gleams that untravell'd world whose margin fades
For ever and forever when I move.
How dull it is to pause, to make an end,
To rust unburnish'd, not to shine in use!
As tho' to breathe were life! Life piled on life
Were all too little, and of one to me
Little remains: but every hour is saved
From that eternal silence, something more,
A bringer of new things; and vile it were
For some three suns to store and hoard myself,
And this gray spirit yearning in desire
To follow knowledge like a sinking star,
Beyond the utmost bound of human thought.

This is my son, mine own Telemachus,
To whom I leave the sceptre and the isle,—
Well-loved of me, discerning to fulfil
This labour, by slow prudence to make mild
A rugged people, and thro' soft degrees
Subdue them to the useful and the good.
Most blameless is he, centred in the sphere
Of common duties, decent not to fail
In offices of tenderness, and pay
Meet adoration to my household gods,
When I am gone. He works his work, I mine.

There lies the port; the vessel puffs her sail:
There gloom the dark, broad seas. My mariners,
Souls that have toil'd, and wrought, and thought with me—
That ever with a frolic welcome took
The thunder and the sunshine, and opposed
Free hearts, free foreheads—you and I are old;
Old age hath yet his honour and his toil;
Death closes all: but something ere the end,
Some work of noble note, may yet be done,
Not unbecoming men that strove with Gods.
The lights begin to twinkle from the rocks:
The long day wanes: the slow moon climbs: the deep
Moans round with many voices. Come, my friends,
'Tis not too late to seek a newer world.
Push off, and sitting well in order smite
The sounding furrows; for my purpose holds
To sail beyond the sunset, and the baths
Of all the western stars, until I die.
It may be that the gulfs will wash us down:
It may be we shall touch the Happy Isles,
And see the great Achilles, whom we knew.
Tho' much is taken, much abides; and tho'
We are not now that strength which in old days
Moved earth and heaven, that which we are, we are;
One equal temper of heroic hearts,
Made weak by time and fate, but strong in will
To strive, to seek, to find, and not to yield.[32]

I think of this log of my voyage as a travel memoir, but were I a librarian, I would find it hard to classify. For whatever it turns out to be, I hope the reader will be a little more

32. *Original Text:* Alfred Lord Tennyson, *Poems*, 2 vols. (Boston: W. D. Ticknor, 1842). PR 5550 E42a Victoria College Library (Toronto). Alfred lord Tennyson, *Works* (London: Macmillan, 1891). Copyright expired.

enlightened and enriched. Methinks, "Some work of noble note, may yet be done."

The Mediterranean sky is indigo this beautiful Sunday morning and there's not a whiff of a cloud to be seen. The sea is deepest aqua. I told the steward this morning that I must have brought good luck for this voyage because we've had superb weather most of the way from Long Beach; however, if the tempest comes between here and Felixstowe, please not to throw me overboard, like the sailors did to Jonah. And yes, I do believe God could make a fish big enough to swallow me.

The Mediterranean does have sperm whales, sighted often in the deeps around Majorca. Whales were correctly thought of in biblical times as dangerous dragons. The lore of whaling is filled with vignettes of the sperm whale's aggressive behavior. Prophesying the deliverance of Israel, Isaiah likened Satan to Leviathan, the sea monster: "In that day, the Lord will punish with his sword, his fierce, great and powerful sword, Leviathan the gliding serpent; . . . He shall slay the monster of the sea" (Isa. 27:1). Dante, in his *Paradise Lost*, also thought of the whale as a monster:

> . . . There Leviathan,
> Hugest of living creatures, in the deep
> Stretched like a promontory sleeps or swims,
> And seems a moving land; and at his gills
> Draws in, and at his breath spouts out the sea.

Thomas Beale's *History of the Sperm Whale* describes a whale's anger on being attacked:

> "Mad with the agonies he endures from these fresh attacks, the infuriated Sperm Whale rolls over and over; he rears his enormous head, and with wide expanded

> jaws snaps at everything about him; he rushes at the boats with his head; they are propelled before him with vast swiftness, and sometimes utterly destroyed."[33]

Although deficient in plankton, the Mediterranean is also still the home of dolphins and the giant loggerhead turtle, an endangered species in the Mediterranean. The turtles return in diminishing numbers every year to the Greek island of Zakinthos, where they struggle among tourists and beachside restaurants for nesting sites.

Today the Cho Yang Atlas is just southwest of the island of Cyprus, that troubled land divided North and South by the Turks and Greeks. It is symbolic of many other places in the world that should live in harmony but where centuries-old hatreds prevail: North and South Korea, Northern Ireland and Britain, North and South Yemen, China and Taiwan; the former Yugoslavia with all of the old nationalism, hatred, intolerance, vindictiveness, and vengeance; Tibet and China; Iran and Iraq; and of course the hopelessly tangled relationships of the entire Middle East. I am not a political scientist or a politician; nor do I care to be. So I am not qualified to offer solutions for peace in these troubled places. But I am convinced that peace can be found one person at a time in the claims of the Christian faith: "My peace I give unto you," declared Jesus, "not as the world gives, give I unto you."

What about this peace of which Jesus speaks? His peace encompasses so much else: freedom from fear, communication with Himself, awe, reverence, discipline and simplicity. Here on this ship I have had the gifts of space and time. Paradoxically, the geographical boundaries, the

33. From Herman Melville's *Moby Dick*, an introduction entitled "Extracts". London: 1851, Reprint: 1994, pp. 17–18. Copyright expired.

physical limitations, the restrictions on communication, have focused my mind and soul on the significant. Here there has been time to be quiet, time to watch the sea in its many moods, time to look at the stars. Even in the seclusion of Arbreux, my country home and retreat in Virginia, my calendar seems to be so full, so few empty pages. Too many activities, worthy though they may be, surrounded by too many valuable things and interesting people.

"It is not merely the trivial which clutters our lives but the important as well," wrote Anne Morrow Lindbergh. "We can have a surfeit of treasures—an excess . . . where one or two would be significant." Here there has been time to ponder the heavens and to stand in awe of the Creator. It has been a temporary seclusion, but I have discovered anew what others have experienced on a long train ride, an ocean voyage, or in retreat by a campfire or a monastery. I believe we need to make room on our calendars for more such retreats. Simplicity of living calls for a balance of physical, intellectual, and spiritual life, space and time to search for lasting significance and beauty, time set aside for solitude and sharing, and closeness to nature. So living, I may thus strengthen my understanding and faith in the intermittency of life. I not only need fellowship with those who think and believe as I do, but I need fellowship with God alone. Thus may I find true peace.

C.G. Jung believed that spiritual health was essential to physical well being: "Among all my patients in the second half of life," he wrote more than a half century ago in *Modern Man in Search of a Soul*, "there has not been one whose problem in the last resort was not that of finding a religious outlook on life. It is safe to say that every one of them fell ill because he had lost that which the living religions of every age have given their followers, and none of them has really been healed who did not regain his religious outlook."[34]

September 27, 1999

We have puffy cotton-ball clouds this morning over the Mediterranean as we approach Sicily and Malta at the toe of Italy's boot. The sea is quietly calm with only a hint of tiny whitecaps here and there. The Third Mate tells me that we are unlikely to see either of the islands as our route takes us through the Malta Strait.

Out on the forecastle this morning I counted nine fishing trawlers, all painted white and easy to see on the horizon. There were several freighters, too, and one ferry ship, gleaming white on the horizon. This afternoon the Mediterranean is as smooth as glass with hardly a ripple. It is still warm, but we are out of the tropics now so the sun does not seem so intense. The mornings are nippy, and in a couple of days we will be turning North into the Atlantic, thus ending the summer wardrobe. The sky has cleared and it should be a good night for watching the stars.

I have been reading Joseph Conrad's *The Heart of Darkness*. Conrad was born in the Russian-dominated area of Poland in 1857. The Russians punished his parents for their Polish nationalist activities and both died while Conrad was still a child. When he was just seventeen, he left Poland for France, where he began his maritime career. He attempted suicide in 1878 but survived to join the British Merchant Navy and spent nearly twenty years at sea before becoming a full-time novelist. In *The Heart of Darkness* he describes the fabled Thames River. In just ten days, the Cho Yang Atlas will dock at Felixstowe somewhere near the

34. C. G. Jung, *Modern Man in Search of a Soul*. New York: Harcourt, Brace, and World, Inc., 1933. Used by permission.

mouth of the Thames. His description will help me view it from a different perspective:

> Forthwith a change came over the waters, and the serenity became less brilliant but more profound. The old river in its broad reach rested unruffled at the decline of day, after ages of good service done to the race that peopled its banks, spread out in the tranquil dignity of a waterway leading to the uttermost ends of the earth. We looked at the venerable stream not in the flush of a short day that comes and departs forever, but in the pacific yet august light of abiding memories. And indeed nothing is easier for a man who has, as the phrase goes, "followed the sea" with reverence and affection, than to evoke the great spirit of the past upon the lower reaches of the Thames.[35]

September 28, 1999

> Where can I go from your Spirit?
> Where can I flee from your Presence?
> If I go up to the heavens, You are there.
> If I make my bed in the depths, You are there.
> If I rise on the wings of the dawn
> If I settle on the far side of the sea
> Even there Your hand will guide me
> Your right hand will hold me fast. (Ps. 139:8–10)

I awoke about 0300 this morning and realized we were going through a storm, with heavy rain and lightning. The rain continued until 0600 and the sky appears to be clearing somewhat here on the western end of the Mediterranean. We are just North of Algiers and South of Majorca

35. Joseph Conrad, *The Heart of Darkness*. London: J. M. Dent, Reprint 1998, p. 4. Copyright expired.

and Barcelona. Captain Mahnke said we will pass through the Pillars of Hercules sometime early tomorrow morning. I made a brief foray out onto the forecastle this morning to "barometer" the weather. There's a South wind blowing, but the temperature is definitely dropping. Well, shouldn't it now that autumn has officially arrived five days ago? And tomorrow we will be heading northward into higher latitudes. I have my winter wardrobe ready.

Among my favorite writers is Britain's F. W. Boreham. Here is an edited essay about Abraham Lincoln that appears in his book *The Temple of Topaz*, written more than a half century ago. Boreham compares Lincoln to Moses, saying Lincoln, too, metaphorically climbed Mt. Sinai.

> The massive personality of Abraham Lincoln is like a granite boulder torn from a rugged hillside. Too gigantic to be localized, he bursts all the bounds of nationality and takes his place in history as a huge cosmopolite. As Edward Stanton so finely exclaimed, in announcing that the last breath of the assassinated President had been drawn, "He belongs henceforth to the ages!"
>
> He was an immense human. . . . Some men are far mightier than their achievement. What they do is great; but what they are is infinitely greater. Abraham Lincoln is the outstanding example of the men of this towering and gigantic cast. The world contains millions of people who know little of American history, and who have but the haziest notions as to the issues at stake in the Civil War, yet upon whose ears the name of Abraham Lincoln falls like an encrusted tradition, like a golden legend, like a brave, inspiring song.
>
> Lincoln climbed Mount Sinai with Moses. . . . Abraham Lincoln's young mother died when he was barely nine. Her husband had to nurse her, close her eyes, make her coffin, and dig her grave. Abraham helped

him carry that melancholy burden from the desolated cabin to its lonely resting-place in the woods. He never forgot that mother of his. "All that I am," he used to say, "my angel-mother made me!" And the memory that lingered the longest was the thought of her as she sat in the old log-cabin teaching him the Ten Commandments. Many a time afterwards, when he was asked how he had found the courage to decline some tempting bribe, or to resist some particularly insidious suggestion, he said that, in the critical hour, he heard his mother's voice repeating once more the old, old words: "I am the Lord thy God; thou shalt have no other gods before Me." He treasured all through life her last words: "I am going away from you, Abraham, and shall not return. I know that you will be a good boy, and you will be kind to your Father. I want you to live as I have taught you, to love your Heavenly Father and to keep His commandments."

President McKinley has told us how, in that fateful hour (when he left Springfield to assume the Presidency), Lincoln received a flag. . . . On its silken folds he read, beautifully worked, the words: "Be strong and of good courage; be not afraid, neither be thou dismayed: For the Lord thy God is with thee whithersoever thou goest. There shall not any man be able to stand before thee all the days of thy life. As I was with Moses, so shall I be with thee.

The greatest grief of his life was the death of his son. As the boy lay dying, Lincoln's reason seemed in peril. Miss Ida Tarbell has told the sad story with great delicacy and judgment. When the dread blow fell, the nurse and the father stood with bowed heads beside the dead boy, and then the nurse, out of her own deep experience of human sorrow and of divine comfort, pointed the weeping President to her Savior.

The work that this private sorrow began, the public sorrow completed. Lincoln had long yearned for a fuller, sweeter, more satisfying faith. "I have been reading the

Beatitudes," he tells a friend, "and can at least claim the blessing that is pronounced upon those who hunger and thirst after righteousness." He was to hunger no longer. A few days before his death he told of the way in which the peace of heaven stole into his heart. "When I left Springfield," he said, not without a thought of the flag and its inscription, "I asked the people to pray for me; I was not a Christian. When I buried my son—the severest trial of my life—I was not a Christian. But when I went to Gettysburg, and saw the graves of thousands of our soldiers, I then and there consecrated myself to Christ." From that moment, Dr. Hill says, the habitual attitude of his mind was expressed in the words: "God be merciful to me, a sinner!" With tears in his eyes he told his friends that he had found the faith that he had longed for. He realized, he said, that his heart was changed, and that he loved the Savior. The President was at the Cross!

Happily, he lived to see the sunshine that followed the storm. He lived to see Peace and Union and Emancipation triumphant. His last hours were spent amidst services of thanksgiving and festivals of rejoicing. One of these celebrations was being held in Ford's Theater at Washington. The President was there, and attracted as much attention as the actors. But his mind was not on the play. Indeed, it was nearly over when he arrived. He leaned forward, talking, under his breath, to Mrs. Lincoln. The war was over, he said, he would like to take her for a tour of the East. They would visit Palestine—would see Gethsemane and Calvary—would walk together the streets of Jeru—! But before the word was finished, a pistol shot—"the maddest pistol—shot in the history of the ages"—rang through the theater. . . .[36]

---

36. The selections included here were taken from F. W. Boreham, *The Temple of Topaz*. London: The Epworth Press, J. Alfred Sharp, First Edition, 1928., pp 25–32. Copyright has expired.

I've just returned from my evening hike on the main deck. The sky tonight is spotlessly clear and the ocean remains calm. We passed a lot of ships today in this main thoroughfare from Europe to Asia. Also, for the first time I saw the vapor trails of an airliner headed from Europe to Africa. I recalled flying that route from Paris and Geneva to such places as Nairobi, Bangui, Dakar, Monrovia, Abijan, Dar-es-Salaam, and I let my imagination run wild. Now comes word from Captain Mahnke that we will not be stopping in LeHavre because of a labor strike in France. That means an earlier arrival in Rotterdam, Hamburg, and Felixstowe. Tomorrow—the Atlantic Ocean!

September 29, 1999

The constellation Ursa Major, with the Big Dipper's handle pointing straight down on Gibraltar, marked our passage this morning through the Pillars of Hercules. Greek mythology says that Hercules, patron Greek god of human labor, flung the Rock of Gibraltar down here on his journey to capture the Red Oxen of Geryones. Across the strait on the Morocco side he tossed another rock, Ceuta. Together these two rocks form the bottleneck to the Mediterranean. It was not until the second century BC that the Romans sailed through these Pillars. Before then, Mediterranean people believed that beyond the Pillars was nothing except chaos, darkness, the Isles of the Hesperides, the lost continent of Atlantis, and a purple river of hellish waters.

Amazingly, the perfect weather continues even here in the temperamental Atlantic Ocean. The sky is cloudless and the sea is calm as we begin our ascent up the Spanish-Portuguese coast toward Lisbon and the Bay of Biscay. For some distance today we were in sight of the Portuguese coast. On one of the towering cliffs overlooking the Atlantic a Moorish fortress castle gleamed in the afternoon sunlight.

Also, I saw the first U.S. Navy ship on this voyage, a supply ship. Captain Mahnke said that earlier we had passed a U. S. aircraft carrier on the port side. All day there have been small vessels along the continental shelf. One small yacht with sails hoisted was far enough off shore to possibly be headed for the Azores. I find myself wondering about the occupants of these small craft so far from land, always with a bit of trepidation; I send up a plea to heaven for their safe landfall.

September 30, 1999

> The sun has one kind of splendor, the moon another and the stars another; and the stars differ from stars in splendor. (1 Cor. 15:41)

"Red sky at morning, sailors take warning." Such is today's admonition as we leave the coast of Spain and head toward England and the Netherlands across the Bay of Biscay. The Third Mate informed me at breakfast that a low-pressure area to our West accounts for the heavy swells this morning. The ship tosses front to rear and side-to-side. Out my starboard window we have just passed two tankers, their main decks invisible behind the spray. The matter-of-fact attitude of our crew, all seasoned sailors, gives reassurance to this novice. This weather, I informed them at breakfast, gives the voyage adventure. They smiled. "Don't mind me," I told them, "I'm a mental case." And they laughed with me.

Overhead a canopy of threatening clouds lying low beneath large spots of blue sky makes for a dramatic sunrise. The sun sends sprays of light through a prism of colors, with the tops of the clouds etched in gold and silver. Somewhere in poetic verse Kipling talked about the sun coming up like thunder; such is the dawn I am witnessing today and every second seems more dramatic than the moment before. Suddenly it breaks through in soaring power and disperses the clouds completely. Over there, beyond my eastern horizon, perhaps in Paris on the Champs d'Elysee, Provence, Arles, or Normandy it is raining this morning. But at least for now, the clouds are gone and the ship bathes in the morning sunshine.

All day the Cho Yang Atlas has ridden the heavy swells. The morning sunshine was eclipsed with heavy clouds in the afternoon. We've passed a number of struggling smaller vessels, and moments ago at dinner the Captain said there was a rescue operation underway nearby for a capsized sailboat. Another ship was closer and the sailor is safe. The whitecaps are the largest I've seen on this voyage. The wind whips spray off the top of each swell and the sun's prism turns it into rainbows. Sometime in the night we will enter the English Channel and tomorrow evening will arrive in Rotterdam. September will have given way to October. Time passes at sea, too, slowly but surely.

October 1, 1999

> I would hurry to my place of shelter far from the tempest and the storm. (Ps. 55:8)

We reached the English Channel this morning and from somewhere in England I heard a British news broadcast: an earthquake in Mexico and a nuclear accident in Japan. The sea, although still choppy, is considerably more placid this morning, with mixed clouds. Our route today will take us past the Isle of Wight, Brighton, and Dover on the port (English) side and the Channel Islands, Cherbourg, and Calais on the starboard (French) side. We have a scheduled arrival time in Rotterdam of 2200.

The fierce sea today gives me a better appreciation of the life of the sailor; they must take the bad and fair weather with equanimity; so must I for the short time remaining for me.

October 2, 1999—Rotterdam

> Rather, as servants of God we commend ourselves in every way: in great endurance; in troubles, hardships and distresses; in beatings, imprisonments and riots; in hard work, sleepless nights and hunger; in purity, understanding, patience and kindness; in the Holy Spirit and in sincere love; in truthful speech and in the power of God; with weapons of righteousness in the right hand and the left; through glory and dishonor, bad report and good report; genuine, yet regarded as imposters; known, yet regarded as unknown; dying and yet we live on; beaten, and yet not killed; sorrowful, yet always rejoicing; poor, yet making many rich; having nothing, and yet possessing everything. (2 Cor. 6:4–10)

A severe storm this morning in the North Sea delays our arrival at port. We are anchored near Rotterdam in swelling seas, awaiting a pilot and a berth at the dock. The steward told me that sometimes the weather is too treacherous for pilot boats; sometimes the harbor pilot is flown by helicopter to the ship. Also, weather conditions are sometimes so dangerous that the pilot will remain on board and go to the ship's next scheduled destination before returning to his home port. Today blustery winds rock the ship and the swells lift and drop it with a noticeable thud. Rain lashes hard against the starboard windows of my cabin. Visibility is nil. It has been eighteen days since the ship left Singapore and the crew seems anxious for shore leave to make phone calls home. In due time the storm will abate and we will be docked. The sea teaches us patience. (My log describing the approach to Rotterdam appears on pages 15–17).

I have spent most of the day editing this log and making minor changes. Now the ship is moving toward the dock area and we will soon be at the berth. Today's storm has passed and the sky is blue with fluffy clouds. The wind is still brisk, reminding me that winter has arrived here in Holland. I think of the daffodils that came from here and are now buried at Arbreux, more than five thousand miles away, awaiting resurrection next spring. The times and seasons pass quickly, as do the seasons of our life. My passage on the Cho Yang Atlas will soon come to an end.

This time next week, I'll be packed to fly home from London's Gatwick Airport. Yes, I've been there, too, long ago, in another passage. Longfellow put it in a poetic line: "Nothing now is left but majesty memory." And I give thanks that most of my memories are majestic.

October 3, 1999

Paul's letter to the church in Ephesus is my meditation this Sunday morning in Holland. His admonition to the Ephesians 2000 years ago is still contemporary.

> . . . to be made new in the attitude of your minds, and to put on a new self, created to be like God in true righteousness and holiness. (Eph. 4:23–24)

It is chilly and overcast this morning in Rotterdam, but the rain and strong winds have ceased and the loading operation is well underway. Rotterdam's port facility is designed to handle the new super-container ships with state-of-the-art computers for loading and unloading.

Overhead cranes here appear to be identical to those at all the other ports. However, here containers are lifted onto a tractor-pulled train of five loader wagons. The tractor/truck is equipped with a computer that tells the driver exactly where to park the wagon beneath the crane's loading dolly. Smaller mobile cranes unload the wagons and stack the containers in numbered rows along painted lines in precision formation like military soldiers mustered for a parade. A master computer tracks each container's location at all times, whether it is stored awaiting shipment, on a loading dolly, a trailer, a crane, or a ship as well as the origin and final destination. To a casual observer, it all seems somewhat miraculous.

We've had mixed weather today and even a few snowflakes this afternoon. Now we're having a thunderstorm and strong winds. But the ship is in port and I will sleep well tonight.

The only video in the ship's library that I cared to watch was *Ben Hur*. So I've been watching it tonight. It won eleven Oscars at the Academy Awards in 1959, forty long years ago, including Best Picture, Best Actor (Charlston Heston), and Best Director (William Wyler). It's too long, so I'll watch the last half tomorrow night.

October 4, 1999

> . . . for it is God who works in you to will and to act according to His good purpose. Do everything without complaining or arguing so that you may become blameless and pure children of God without fault in a crooked and depraved generation, in which you shine like stars in the universe, as you hold out the word of life." (Phil. 2:13–16)

I am still reading Paul's epistles and when I read that verse last night, I thought—Wow! Shining like stars in the universe? That has a new meaning for me now, having gazed at the canopy of heaven several nights at sea when the sky was cloudless and there were no sounds except the waves of the ocean. But, oh, what a magnificence . . . and obligation! Especially in contrast with the darkness of the world, surely for many struggling with depression, looking for the light of a smile, for any glint of joy and laughter, for any hint of love that may be left in the world. No wonder Jesus said "Love one another." C. S. Lewis wrote that we are commanded to love even the most unlovable because in eternity they may appear as beings so dazzling we cannot look upon them—shining like stars?

Loading at the Rotterdam dock has been delayed because of heavy rainstorms overnight. Each compartment's hold on the ship will store almost as many containers as the area above it on the main deck. Normally, when the hold is filled, a gigantic lid seals the hold. When the heavy rains came, several holds were still exposed and filled with water. All but one have now been pumped dry and sealed. So we hope to be underway to Hamburg by noon. The ten-hour trek to Hamburg takes us along the coast of Holland to the West of the Frisian Islands that form the outer banks of the Zuider Zee, famous in folklore. We will enter the Elbe River and go inland a few miles past Bremerhaven to Hamburg. The port of Bremerhaven is familiar to almost any veteran who may have been posted in Belgium, Germany, France, or Holland. It was through this port that all military posts were supplied and all household goods and personal vehicles were shipped.

The Karmann-Ghia Volkswagen that took me all over Germany in those days was shipped home to America from

Bremerhaven. I named her Gretchen and fell passionately in love with her. She was faithful and never once refused to take me where I wanted or needed to go. Alas, she had an ignominious end. I traded her for a Volkswagen Beetle but a friend bought her from the dealer. She had increased in value to more than I had paid for her four years earlier. On a fateful afternoon in 1975, she was smashed from the sky as an airborne eighteen wheeler left a freeway in Little Rock, Arkansas and capsized on top of her in a parking lot. More majesty memories flood in as I recall the good times with her in Deutschland with dear friends; Wiesbaden, where I lived; Bavaria, with Octoberfests, schnitzel, wurst, hanchen mit essig und pommes frites (chicken with vinegar and French fries); and the magic of castles on the Rhine. I thought of myself as poor then but how rich I was then—and now—with memories!

We had another slight delay when one of the containers was mishandled and locked sideways. I watched with empathy for the crane operators and loaders atop the containers as they struggled with unlocking the miscreant. Finally, the container slipped loose and was able to be reloaded and locked properly in place.

The Third Mate told me that containers are packed for safety so that contents are properly secured from the elements and balanced to prevent movement and friction while at sea. According to Peter Nichols, writing in *Sea Change*, sometimes containers are thrown while in rough seas. However, from my observation, I believe this is a rare event because of the precautions taken while loading.

We departed Rotterdam at 1200. Ships I listed in the harbor were the Trein Maersk, Linda Maersk, Sealand Atlantic New York, HMS Portugal, Sten Tor, Elbe, Hanjin Washington, Courage, the ferry Rosebay, and tankers

Margaron, Vlumen, Veghel, and Hein. Leaving the harbor, I counted fourteen large ships at anchor offshore awaiting berths; a busy seaport is Rotterdam!

A ship's agent in Rotterdam brought aboard current issues of the *Wall Street Journal* and London's *Financial Times*. These were the first newspapers I had read for a month and a half. I was surprised to find that there was not a peep of news in either one of them about the United States. However, the *Financial Times* had a full-page lead story examining the world's supply of water and stating that the world is dangerously short, predicting a global crisis in just twenty years. According to Philip Ball, water is a liquid far more valuable than oil and is likely to run out sooner. After all the water I've seen for the past six weeks, imagine my incredulity!

According to Ball, fresh water is constantly renewed by nature's cycles, but at any instant less than 100th of one percent of the planet's surface water is suitable and available for human use. Seawater is of virtually no value for direct human use and its salt content makes it toxic to many living organisms. To remove the salt is almost prohibitively expensive and only wealthy countries conduct large-scale desalinization to obtain fresh water. Meanwhile, available sources of fresh water are shrinking because of pollution. Ball's alarmist views are sure to help sell his book *H20, A Biography of Water*. The comments that got my attention were "The bitter irony is that our planet is two thirds blue," and "We need to learn to value water, to see it not as a repository for waste or a limitless commodity that can be flushed down the pan, but as a kind of blue gold."

I've had another several moments of serendipity! From the forward windows of the library and officers' dayroom just below the bridge, I watched as the ship headed directly into a storm with blue sky and sunshine to our aft. A rainbow with the most intensive colors arched directly over the Cho Yang Atlas and became more brilliant as we neared the storm. It remained for a full fifteen minutes, terminating directly on either side of the ship and magnifying itself into a double rainbow. I lamented that my camera has malfunctioned; but the scene is permanently implanted on my memory.

We are being pushed by a strong aft wind up the European coast toward Hamburg. The pilot who came on board to help us negotiate the Elbe River into Hamburg said this would speed our arrival time. Again we have very choppy seas. Looking out the cabin windows toward the horizon you sense that the ship is in a canyon and you are looking uphill. In good weather at sea, you sense that you are looking downhill to the horizon's jumping off place. We are near enough to the offshore islands to see them while buoys mark the edge of the continental shelf for safety of large vessels.

After dinner tonight I watched the last half of *Ben Hur*. I had forgotten how it ended. Miriam and Tirzah, the mother and sister of Judah Ben Hur, are healed of their leprosy just at the moment of Jesus' death upon the cross. The movie faithfully reproduces the storm that took place at the moment of His death and as I watched this scene, we were going through a real storm at sea. It made the ending of the movie even more dramatic.

October 5, 1999—Hamburg

> Or take ships as an example. Although they are so large and are driven by strong winds, they are steered by a very small rudder wherever the pilot wants to go. (James 3:4)

James compared a ship's rudder with the tongue, with emphasis on taming it. Yesterday afternoon the ship was driven by strong winds for sure. And all along I kept wondering, with the strong winds and turbulent seas, why I had not left the ship in Rotterdam and boarded a ferry to Felixstowe, thus gaining an extra day in London. But then I thought: "I would have missed that magnificent rainbow!" There was my pot of gold.

We docked in Hamburg this morning at 0600. The cranes are on the port side of the ship this time and so I can watch the harbor traffic from my cabin window.

Another change in schedule. Captain Mahnke informed me that we will go to LeHavre before Felixstowe. It means an extra two days on the ship, with only one day in London. The turnaround in LeHavre will be a short fifteen hours, subject to change! Meanwhile, more adventure at sea!

The first thing I noticed this morning when I looked over the skyline of Hamburg with my binoculars was the number of church steeples in this industrial city. I counted eleven from my cabin windows. Those steeples make a powerful statement, just by being there still. No matter that perhaps only a handful of faithful believers still worship there, Christianity survives. These few are the remnant Jesus called the salt of the earth, giving it flavor, and the light of the world, reflecting the glow of His light.

When I focus my binoculars at the top of the steeples of these churches, I see that each one is capped with a cross. I rack my brain to express my reaction to seeing them, but nothing fills the space in my mind but the cross itself, and the cross is all I need. Malcolm Muggeridge, looking back over his long life, saw the cross as the symbol of significance of human pain and affliction and in the end, the one thing that gave his life meaning:

> Contrary to what might be expected, I look back on experiences that at the time seemed especially desolating and painful. I now look back on them with particular satisfaction. Indeed, I can say with complete truthfulness that everything I have learned in my seventy-five years in this world, everything that has truly enhanced and enlightened my existence has been through affliction and not through happiness whether pursued or attained. In other words, I say this, if it were to be possible to eliminate affliction from our earthly existence by means of some drug or other medical mumbo-jumbo, the result would not be to make life delectable, but to make it banal and trivial to be endurable. This, of course, is what the cross signifies and it is the cross, more than anything else, that has called me inexorably to Christ.[37]

Muggeridge's testimony reminds me of the apostle Paul's words to the church at Rome which have always reverberated with meaning for me:

> Not only so, but we rejoice in our sufferings, because we know that suffering produces perseverance; perseverance, character; and character, hope. And hope does not disappoint us, because God has poured out His love into our hearts by the Holy Spirit, whom He has given us. (Rom. 5:3–5)

It has been a sunny, delightful day in Hamburg. There's been more hustle and bustle around and aboard the ship

37. Malcolm Muggeridge, *A Twentieth-Century Testimony.* Nashville: Thomas Nelson, 1978, p. 72. Used by permission.

than usual because this is where the ship is provisioned for the entire round-trip trek to Asia and America. A crane lifted a huge load of food, gas canisters, diesel oil, and other supplies onto the platform aft of the cooking galley. The crew hustled to stow it. Two of the German crew will remain here for home leave, and their replacements were welcomed aboard. The Captain is welcoming and hosting his family tonight. Tomorrow the ship will begin another long round trip three-quarters of the way around the world. I admire and salute their dedication, sacrifice, and professionalism. The Captain said today that few professions "on the ground" allowed such teamwork and esprit-de-corps for the professional. I agree. And the work they do is important and needed. Theirs is a necessary link in the chain of commerce that feeds, clothes, and provisions the whole world and everybody in it. They have justifiable reason to be proud indeed. And I feel very privileged to have been an observer for these few weeks aboard.

October 6, 1999

> But in your hearts set about Christ as Lord. Always be prepared to give an answer to everyone who asks you to give the reason for the hope that you have. But do this with gentleness and respect . . . so that in all things God may be praised through Jesus Christ. To Him be the glory and the power for ever and ever. Amen. (1 Pet. 3:5; 4:11).

Clear skies and sunshine this morning to begin our trek to LeHavre, pulling away from the dock at 0830. But windy! The sailing time to LeHavre is about twenty hours. We came into Hamburg on the Elbe River in darkness. Leaving now by daylight in splendid weather permits excellent views of the German countryside and the small villages with pastoral scenes and sheep grazing on the dikes, recalling memories of my years living in Deutschland.

Two passengers joined us in Hamburg, so I will have brief opportunity to make new friends. They come from Stuttgart and Munich. We passed the German welcome center and I was invited on the bridge where a sound system on shore played the last stanza of the German national anthem. Captain Mahnke explained that singing or playing the first two stanzas of the national anthem after the war was unacceptable to Americans, who misinterpreted the nationalistic theme to mean "Germany above all others," and it was consequently forbidden.

Hamburg's harbor is approximately 100 miles inland from the sea, so the going is slow, with small pleasure craft, fishing trawlers, pilot boats, and ferries along the river. A cloud of gulls trailed one of the fishing trawlers, culling for fish, recalling similar scenes when I lived near the sea at Wakkanai, Japan. Also, we passed a tall-masted sailing ship named Fryderyk Chopin, no doubt a national ship of Poland. What national pride in a native genius who gave the world Nocturnes and Polonaises to summon angels. The ship was spectacular and worthy of his name. Still later, another very large yacht under full sail with three masts was on my starboard side, but it was too far away to detect the name. I have a new appreciation for the skills it must take to navigate a vessel of this size under full sail out to sea. The ship looked so vulnerable and I felt so safe and secure aboard the Cho Yang Atlas!

I must admit to a bit of disappointment that our ship was not going directly from Hamburg to Felixstowe as planned. As it is, we will go now to LeHavre and back to Felixstowe, which will leave only one day in London. But perhaps it will be long enough for me to find the books I'm hoping to find, then set my mind on flying home, ending this odyssey. So comes the end of another day at sea with a spectacular sunset. I give thanks and close down my laptop and say to myself "schlafen gute" (sleep well).

October 7, 1999

> Then I looked and heard the voice of many angels, numbering thousands upon thousands, and ten thousands upon ten thousands. They encircled the throne and the living creatures and the elders. In a loud voice they sang:
>
> Worthy is the Lamb, who was slain, to receive power and wealth and wisdom and strength and honor and glory and praise!
>
> Then I heard every creature in heaven and on earth and under the earth and on the sea, and all that is in them, singing:
>
> To Him who sits on the throne and to the Lamb be praise and honor and glory and power, forever and ever! (Rev. 5:11–13)

Today was the day I was scheduled to depart the ship but I am on my way to LeHavre. With the earlier schedule, having bypassed LeHavre, I would have been in London yesterday. But then late yesterday came word of a serious train accident in London. I may have been spared much anxiety and stress with transportation disruptions. I give thanks for delays and I learn patience. "All things work together for good," wrote the apostle Paul.

For more than an hour now, I have been seeing the lights of the coast of Dover, directly opposite Calais on the French coast, as we make our way again into the English Channel. Directly below us somewhere is that infamous tunnel that joins Britain and France.

This morning we were given a tour of the diesel plant that is the heartbeat of this ship. You descend multiple stairways from the hospital-clean computerized control room past the massive diesel engines, past the mammoth propeller and on to the steering operation center that controls the rudder. Along the way are the water treatment plant that sterilizes water taken from the sea, an incinerator for garbage and trash disposal, and an electric generating plant. A tunnel track beneath the outside walkway of the main deck provides access to the water, electrical, and communications equipment completely around the ship. The whole complex is scrupulously clean.

October 8, 1999—LeHavre

We arrived in LeHavre at 2100. The harbor seems strangely quiet, no doubt because of the labor strike under way here. Captain Mahnke informs me that he has no definite schedule for sailing, so I will be departing soon. I will leave the Cho Yang Atlas because the labor strike in France may delay the ship's departure for Felixstowe further. I will either go to Calais and take the train through the Eurotunnel to London or fly from LeHavre to London. So another adventure!

October 9, 1999—London-Gatwick

Yesterday I said *bon voyage* to my friends on the Cho Yang Atlas and flew to London-Gatwick via Air France from LeHavre as the most expeditious means of transportation.

I arrived in London at 0745, after a flight through heavy clouds and turbulent winds nearly all the way. It was exhilarating to discover that I was only a short distance from The Renaissance Gatwick Hotel, where I had made reservations three months ago. After an exuberant and filling

English breakfast, I set out for London on the Gatwick Express. The first place I wanted to go was Charing Cross Road to find out-of-print books. The exit from Charing Cross tube station brought me up immediately in front of Lord Nelson's colossal lions. Suddenly, in my reveries I was again in Kenya at Karen, the place named for Baroness Blixen, and remembering my visit to Denys Fitch Hatton's grave. I recalled that Karen Blixen in *Out of Africa* wrote of hearing that lions came to the grave of Denys Fitch Hatton on a hill near the farm in Kenya:

> The Masai . . . have reported . . . that many times, at sunrise and sunset, they have seen lions on Finch-Hatton's grave in the Hills. A lion and a lioness have come there, and stood, or lain, on the grave for a long time. . . . It was fit and decorous that the lions should come to Denys's grave and make him an African monument. "And renowned be thy grave." Lord Nelson himself, I reflected, in Trafalgar Square, has his lions made only out of stone.[38]

I also went to Harrods to buy Christmas gifts and to have lunch in the famous food halls. Today, I went back to Sir Christopher Wren's St. Paul's Cathedral. In the courtyard is a memorial to the Old St. Paul's Cross. I sat down on the pavement and copied these engraved words:

> On this plot of ground stood of old St Paul's Cross where amid such scenes of good and evil as make up human affairs the conscience of the church and nation through five centuries found public utterance.

38. Karen Blixen (Isac Dineson), *Out of Africa*. London, Penguin Books, 1937, p. 308. Used by permission.

While I was copying these words, John Martin, a professor at Cambridge University and director of Cambridge Christian Heritage, walked by and stopped to say that just a short while before, he himself had sat and copied those same words. For the millennium celebration, he is directing walking tours of London. He shared with me some materials he had collected about the witness of early Christian leaders, including the Wesleys.

At the John Wesley Statue in St. Paul's churchyard are inscribed these words:

> From 1738 . . . speaking continually of Jesus Christ; laying on Him only as the foundation of the whole building, making Him all in all, the first and the last; preaching only on this plan, "the Kingdom of God is at hand, repent ye and believe the Gospel", the Word of God ran as fire among the stubble; it was glorified more and more; multitudes crying out, "What must we do to be saved?" and after witnessed, "By grace we are saved through faith."

"Historians say that the effect of Wesley's evangelical preaching saved England from an experience like the French Revolution," wrote John Martin. "He is often called, 'the greatest Englishman.'"[39]

I went to Skoob's Bookstore because it advertises itself as the "best secondhand bookstore in London." I didn't find the books I had hoped to find, but added a couple of new old books to my collection. Then I set out to stroll down Bond Street and Saville Row, famous for its haberdasheries to wealthy gentlemen. But the crushing mobs of early Christmas shoppers sent me scurrying underground and

39. John Martin, Notes: *City Christian Heritage Walks.* Cambridge: Round Street Vestry, 1999. Quote is in the public domain.

back to Victoria Station to catch the Gatwick Express and to return to my hotel.

Tomorrow, I will fly home to America. After two days of rubbing elbows with thousands of people on the streets of London and in the Underground, I look forward to the peace and solitude of Arbreux, whence I will try to distill this journey into something my mind can contain. I will have a lot of sorting to do.

October 11, 1999—Arbreux

Home is the Sailor, Home from the Sea....

I came home to Arbreux today following yesterday's long flight from London. I found the dogwoods are the color of oxblood, the birches are golden as wheat, and the oaks are shades of cinnamon and old leather. When I left, summer was halcyon, and fields were tinged in shades of tan because of the drought. But rains in my absence have turned the fields to emerald.

Time passes. In these hills the seasons pass in review like squadrons in a long parade, some dressed more regal than others but all marching in cadence to the Creator's certain drumbeat. At sea, the seasons pass, too, in shadowed tones, not so richly adorned as these mountains. For a while at least, I'll live consciously in both worlds—a mountain man and a sailor. I give thanks for my several worlds and the multicolored seasons of my life.

Debarkation

Readers will question why this book was written and what motivated me to devote so much time, energy and resources to bring it into print. This same question intrigues me as I reflect on the passage of time aboard ship and other travels of body and soul in the past few years. The answer involves the mystical notion which the apostle Paul spoke of in 2 Corinthians 5:17: "Therefore if any man be in Christ, he is a new creature: old things are passed away; behold, all things are become new."

Paul's definition of a Christian is a man *in Christ* who has become a new creation. Not merely is he improved or reformed; he is remade and remolded into someone different altogether than he was before. The old has passed away . . . the new has come. Everything he sees in the physical world is changed and redeemed to new beauty and possibility. Such was the world I purposed to look upon as I rode the ocean waves of the planet. At the same time I was absorbed in thought and prayer about what gives my life and my world meaning. John Reid, writing in an expository to 2 Corinthians, helped me in my quest:

> Meaning comes back into a situation which otherwise is like a code message without the key, or a stained-glass window without the light to reveal its color or significance. No one who has not submitted himself to the experience of God in Christ is competent to make a pronouncement on the world and on human life. Such an experience not only makes the world new, but adds to the world its most vital element. The knowledge of Christ, and the experience of love, like the acquisition of a new and transforming friendship, enrich and interpret all other experience.[40]

40. John Reid, Exposition on II Corinthians 5:17, in *The Interpreter's Bible*. Nashville: Abingdon Press, 1953, p. 338–339. Used by permission.

Because I had been blessed with what I believed to be a unique passage, I felt compelled to log my journey with the most descriptive words I could muster. This was an adventure centered in the Christian faith. Faith in Christ is not something added to life to make it more livable. It is rather a mystical deliverance without which there is no hope. It is not of our doing, but of God's alone. Christian belief is not merely preferable to other forms of belief or unbelief; it is literally a matter of life and death. We enter by faith into the fellowship of the spirit of Christ and we become alive from the dead.

As we continue to live in His fellowship this new life becomes progressively more real and abundant. To be *in Christ* is to be delivered from a meaningless existence and at last to live, resurrected from the dead emptiness of all once thought to be living. All of nature and God's creation bursts forth in rapturous applause; the soul has discovered that *God is love.* This exceedingly good news must be shared else the very stones will cry out.

Crew List—Cho Yang Atlas

Long Beach, California to Felixstowe, England
August 24, 1999 to October 7, 1999

Captain Ulf E. Mahnke	Master
Hans H. Werner	Chief Officer
Manuelito A. DelaLuna	2nd Officer
Joel C. Semino	3rd Officer
Peter Pieper	Chief Engineer
Friedrich Knorek	2nd Engineer
Alfonso Labio	3rd Engineer
Rey Cajita	Electrician
Jens Kohler	Ship's Mechanic
Tamaeu Tauro	Bosun
Teaero Kinta	AB 5
Viriteti Kabuta	AB 5
Makauau Toom	AB 5
Bwaauto Tebikau	AB 3–4
Maere Kaumai	AB 3–4
Kaitara Maan	MM 5
Timwemwe Reo	MM 5
Teuaia Brechtefeld	MM 5
Jose Goli	Cook
Kaiteie Teaotai	QS 5
Biita Bubutei	QSC 1

End Notes:

The Fair Use Section [107] of the 1976 Copyright Law provides for quotations of excerpts from previously published works for the purpose of illumination or comment without permission. Most of the quotations used in this book could be thus categorized. Nevertheless, a concerted effort was made to obtain permission for all quotations used. In some instances the copyright had expired or the copyright owner could not be established. The author wishes to express his appreciation to the authors and publishers for all material used.

To order additional copies of

Pondering Another Passage

Have your credit card ready and call

(877)421-READ (7323)

or send $10.00 each, plus $3.95* S&H to

WinePress Publishing
PO Box 428
Enumclaw, WA 98022

*add $1.00 S&H for each additional book ordered